THE
PRAYER FACTOR

THE
PRAYER
FACTOR

Sammy Tippit

Scripture Press

Amersham-on-the-Hill, Bucks HP6 6JQ, England

© 1988 The Moody Bible Institute of Chicago

First British edition 1989

ISBN 0 946515 82 4

Designed and printed in Great Britain for
SCRIPTURE PRESS FOUNDATION (UK) LTD
Raans Road, Amersham-on-the-Hill, Bucks HP6 6JQ by
Nuprint Ltd, 30b Station Road, Harpenden, Herts AL5 4SE

To Titus,
who taught me to weep for souls

Contents

Part 1: Motivation for Prayer

Part 2: Instruction for Prayer

Part 3: Prayer and Spiritual Awakening

Foreword

You can't read what Sammy Tippit has to say about prayer without sensing that he is a man who knows what he's talking about.

The success of his dynamic, evangelistic preaching all over the world—from the communist bloc to India, Africa, Western Europe, and the United States—evidences effectual, fervent prayer.

The Prayer Factor is written by a man who has learned the discipline of spending long blocks of time communing with his God. Sammy Tippit walks us through Motivation for Prayer, Instruction for Prayer, and Prayer and Spiritual Awakening.

This is not a devotional work, although you'll find it devotional. This is not an inspirational work, although there is more than enough solid biblical content to allow you to use it for just that.

Rather, this is a primer for prayer. If you struggle with that area of your relationship to God, or if you simply want to enhance an already healthy prayer life, this is the prescription for you.

If you fear *The Prayer Factor* might be a dry thesis on a complex doctrine, I encourage you to just try a few riveting pages. You won't want to miss a word.

DR. JOSEPH M. STOWELL, PRESIDENT
MOODY BIBLE INSTITUTE

Part 1
Motivation for Prayer

Men ought always to pray. (Luke 18:1, KJV)

Trouble and prayer are closely related to each other. Prayer is of great value to trouble. Trouble often drives men to God in prayer, while prayer is but the voice of men in trouble.

(E. M. Bounds, *The Essentials of Prayer* [Baker, 1987])

The times of refreshing from the presence of the Lord have at last dawned upon our land. Everywhere there are signs of aroused activity and increased earnestness. A spirit of prayer is visiting our churches. . . . The first breath of the rushing mighty wind is already discerned, while on the rising of evangelists the tongue of fire has evidently descended.

(C. H. Spurgeon, *The New Park Street Pulpit* [1859])

Now to Him who is able to do exceeding abundantly beyond all that we ask or think, according to the power that works within us, to Him be the glory in the church and in Christ Jesus to all generations forever and ever. Amen.

(Ephesians 3:20-21)

1

The Victory of Prayer

Early in my Christian life God brought me in contact with men of prayer. These men came from various occupations—laymen, pastors, and evangelists. They were not necessarily considered the most successful in their churches and communities, neither did they pastor the largest churches or receive the largest salaries.

They did possess, however, a Christian's most valuable characteristic: a heart yielded to God. They were on fire with the love of Jesus. They did not equate victory with the world's standard of success; they saw victory as obedience to the will of God.

One of these men was Pastor L. L. Morris. Pastor Morris shepherded a small Baptist church in Monroe, Louisiana. In the late 1960s he asked me to preach in evangelistic meetings in his church.

A few weeks before the meetings began I grew discouraged. Reaching the people seemed impossible. The church and community possessed little interest in spiritual matters. The Vietnam War raged on. Young people were rejecting the values of their elders. Drugs and Eastern mysticism were capturing young people. Racial tensions plagued the schools. Worldly standards were creeping into churches. I felt defeated and helpless.

Pastor Morris asked me to attend a prayer session with the young people. Only a few attended. I told Pastor Morris, "I believe we ought to cancel the evangelistic meetings. There is no interest. We will be wasting my time, your time, and the church's time."

I will never forget his response. With a twinkle in his eye he said, "I've been praying. God has given me assurance that He is going to do something special during these meetings."

I shook my head and said, "OK, but I will have to go on your faith."

I preached the first evening. There was absolutely no response. I looked at Pastor Morris as if to say, "I told you so."

He smiled and said, "I've been praying. It will be OK."

On Thursday night I preached to about fifty people. There seemed to be no effect on the congregation. However, at the time of invitation one of the church leaders came forward and prayed with Pastor Morris. He then came to the pulpit with tears in his eyes and asked the church to forgive him. He confessed that he had failed the young people by being a poor example. He said that God had now freed him of his alcohol problem. He then asked the church to pray for him.

Something wonderful happened that moment. A spirit of brokenness and prayer swept the congregation. The altar was filled with people confessing sin and seeking God's righteousness. On Friday evening the church was nearly full.

One of the church members had a daughter who had been arrested twice for the sale and use of marijuana and other drugs. She was facing a possible thirty-year prison sentence. She had been in drug-rehabilitation centers, but she had found no cure. She was deeply involved in the occult.

My wife, Tex, visited her and shared the gospel with her. She came to the services and was stunned by the truth of God's Word. After the service one evening she asked Jesus to come into her life and set her free from her slavery to drugs. The authorities later were so impressed by the change in her life that they released her to the custody of my wife and me.

By Sunday evening there was not room for the crowds. Pastor Morris said, "I've been praying, and I believe we ought to extend these meetings another week." I knew not to argue. We moved from the church to the university campus. The first building we secured was also not sufficient for the crowds. We moved to a larger building. It was not sufficient, either.

Pastor Morris said to Ray Mears, the worship leader, and me, "I've been praying. I think we ought to talk to the former Louisiana governor. He owns the local television station, and we should ask him for time on television to tell what God is doing in our city."

I said skeptically, "I don't think he will help us."

But Pastor Morris said, "I've been praying, and God will prepare his heart."

The governor was not only receptive to us, but he gave us two fifteen-minute television spots to tell what God was doing in Monroe. Then he said, "You're having problems with lack of space. Do you think that the civic center would be big enough?"

Shocked, I said, "Yes, sir."

He telephoned the mayor. I was amazed when I heard him say, "I have some young men in my office who are doing something positive in our community. They need larger facilities. I would like for you to donate the civic center to them free of charge."

The mayor agreed.

I walked out of his office that day humbled at the greatness of God. I looked over at Pastor Morris. He said nothing, but he had a smile on his face. I realized in that moment one of the great truths of the Christian life: *Victory does not come from our magnificent schemes, expert publicity, or financial holdings, but victory comes from the Lord*. Pastor Morris had learned that lesson years before, and it drove him to be a faithful, humble man of prayer.

During that time a room was set aside for prayer. Twenty-four hours a day young people could be found in that room praying. The spirit of prayer was so great that occasionally people were unable to eat.

The meetings that began with forty to fifty people concluded with around three thousand. Both black and white students involved in racial tension were converted to Christ, and they asked each other's forgiveness. I was interviewed on the evening news several times. Several newspaper articles were written about the visitation of God's Spirit upon the youth of Monroe, Louisiana.

Out of this I was thrust into a ministry of evangelism. Although Pastor Morris has since gone to be in the presence of the Lord, I will never forget his words, "I've been praying." His life was a testimony to a God who hears and answers prayer.

THE ABSENCE OF VICTORY IN OUR SOCIETY

Every generation must have a fresh touch of God; otherwise the gospel becomes perverted. Religious manipulators use the name of Jesus for their own selfish motives, and the gospel has no effect on the lives of people or on society as a whole.

This generation has been plagued with religious manipulators. The evangelical church has become accustomed to the preachers of "faith" begging for money rather than trusting God. It has become the norm rather than the exception.

We speak of success and prosperity rather than the victory of the cross. We have produced a generation of Christians who believe that diamonds and expensive cars are proof of a successful Christian life. We have forgotten that we are called to be like Jesus. And Jesus did not think in terms of outward success; He lived only with the thought of obedience. His joy was to do the will of the Father.

A cloud of darkness hangs over much of the church. Evangelical Christians in America have recently come through one of the most embarrassing periods in their history. Every major newspaper in the United States has published stories of the sins and perversions of Christians. Many Christians wait with deep concern, wondering who will be the next leader exposed for his or her sin. Others flaunt their sins by marrying, divorcing, and remarrying, while at the same time writing their books, pastoring their churches, and producing their record albums. They proclaim that they have understood forgiveness in a new way. Unfortunately, it is a forgiveness without repentance that does not produce holiness.

The world looks and laughs. They sneer at the coercive methods of fund-raising used by many evangelicals. The church has become the brunt of jokes rather than the light of the world and the salt of the earth.

But thousands of years before this scandal hit America, a greater scandal hit heaven. That scandal was pride in the hearts of religious manipulators. Pride always precedes a fall because God is opposed to the proud.

Pride has been at the root of man's sin for thousands of years. It was pride that caused Lucifer to be lifted up in his heart. It was pride that fostered a rebellion against God. As a result Lucifer was cast out of heaven. And now he continually encourages pride in the hearts of men and women so that they will join him in his rebellion. He is often subtle in his attempts. He dresses pride in many different robes— robes of self-righteousness, of cultural and racial pride, and of spiritual arrogance. When one of God's children clothes himself with one of these robes, there is scandal in heaven. And in a matter of time scandal in heaven becomes scandal on earth. The secret sin of pride is ultimately exposed by God's light. The only robe for the child of God is Christ's righteousness and grace—the robe of the humble heart.

The first sign that scandal has hit heaven is prayerlessness—when the sweet fragrance of the prayers of God's people cease to ascend to His throne. The church begins to depend upon technology and talent, substituting man's ingenuity for God's power. The church begins to run on bureaucracy rather than on the bended knee.

When prayer is replaced by form and function the church becomes spiritually anemic. Andrew Murray stated, "Prayer is the pulse of life; by it the doctor can tell what is the condition of the heart. The sin of prayerlessness is a proof for the ordinary Christian or minister that the life of God in the soul is in deadly sickness and weakness."[1]

The church must recapture her distinctive. She is not built upon manipulation and money. She is built upon the might of God. If the church is to be light in this perverse generation, she must humble herself and pray. She must understand that victory comes from her knees.

THE POTENTIAL FOR VICTORY IN CHRIST

Prayer is the manifestation of a humble heart. Humility secures the grace of God and our victory. The humble heart is not an option; it is a necessity. E. M. Bounds, who well understood the life of prayer, said, "God puts a great price on humility. . . . That which brings the praying soul near to God is humility of heart. That which gives wings to prayer is lowliness of mind. It gives access to God when other qualities fail."[2]

Victory flows from the heart of humility *because* the grace of God is applied. When we understand this principle our whole perspective changes. And the greatest example of this principle is the Lord Jesus. Immediately before going to the Garden of Gethsemane and on to Calvary, Jesus told His

1. Andrew Murray, *The Prayer Life* (Springdale, Pa.: Whitaker House, 1987), p. 15.
2. E. M. Bounds, *The Essentials of Prayer* (Grand Rapids: Baker, 1987), p. 21.

disciples, "These things I have spoken to you, that in Me you may have peace. In the world you have tribulation, but take courage; I have overcome the world" (John 16:33).

Jesus spoke of victory immediately before praying and prior to seeming defeat. These words must have puzzled His disciples when He died. How could victory come from failure? How could victory come from death? How could victory come from the despised cross?

But Jesus knew the heart of the Father. And out of this knowledge He endured the cross "for the joy set before Him" (Hebrews 12:2). Philippians 2:8-9 says, "He *humbled* Himself by becoming obedient to the point of death, even death on a cross. Therefore also God highly *exalted* Him, and bestowed on Him the name which is above every name" (emphasis added).

Jesus knew humiliation preceded exaltation. The essence of His life was humility. And although He exists in eternity (past, present, and future) as God, He chose to humble Himself by becoming man. As a man He spent much time in prayer. He did nothing on His own initiative; He depended on the Father for all things. His humility was exemplified by His prayer life.

Jesus bids us to join Him in the school of prayer. In this school we learn the way of victory that is desperately needed in our personal lives, our communities, and our generation. Every great man and woman of God throughout history has been trained and equipped in this school.

The Holy Spirit, the school's headmaster, establishes our course of training. He has given us professors Law and Failure as tutors. Professor Law teaches us the standard of God; Professor Failure teaches us that we cannot reach that standard. We are led to the startling fact that without Jesus we can do nothing.

Moses enrolled in the school of prayer and became mighty in spirit. Few in the history of man equal Scripture's assessment of Moses. He was described as: the servant of the Lord (Deuteronomy 34:5), the greatest prophet in Israel

(Deuteronomy 34:10), the friend of God (Exodus 33:11), and the most humble man in his generation (Numbers 12:3).

Moses was given such an appraisal, however, only after his completion of the school of prayer. Moses' life can be divided into three forty-year periods. The first period was spent in the Egyptian schools. There he learned self-sufficiency. He became mighty in the eyes of the world—commander in chief of one of the mightiest military forces in the world.

Yet Moses was unable to help his own countrymen. He needed to come under the tutorship of Professor Failure before he could become God's man. He had to first discover that his human strength and ability could never free his brothers and sisters from their bondage.

Moses killed an Egyptian and fled in fear to the land of Midian. The mighty soldier became a poor shepherd. He who had much was left with little. But it was there that God met with him. God does not build His kingdom on the might of men and women but in humble hearts.

A businessman once said to me, "In business I am taught to think big. In the kingdom of God, however, I am taught to think small." That man understood the nature of God's kingdom. God blesses a heart that has tasted failure and defeat. He blesses a hurting heart. God uses unimportant people, people that have learned that Professor Failure turns our eyes Godward. They have learned that it is only when they become *nothing* that God can become *everything*. As a result of this lesson they are enabled to see the glory of God.

When Jesus came to establish His kingdom on the earth, He began with insignificant people. He chose Peter, a fisherman, and Matthew, a tax collector. He chose the nobodies of the world, and He began to establish His kingdom in their hearts. When He unveiled the manifesto of His kingdom, He said, "Blessed are the poor in spirit, for theirs is the kingdom of heaven" (Matthew 5:3).

This generation must learn that victory comes from the Lord, not from our own abilities. We have attempted to convert the world with the methods of the world. We have learned the ways of Hollywood and the power of psychological and emotional manipulation. But we have been left defeated.

We must now enroll in God's school and learn His method. The method of God is simple, humble, and holy praying men and women. God can do more with a defeated Moses in the desert than He can with a slick, powerful Moses in Egypt. God is looking for broken men and women who will seek His face.

E. M. Bounds describes this principle by stating, "Humility is an indispensable requisite of true prayer. It must be an attribute, or characteristic of prayer. Humility must be in the praying character as light is in the sun. Prayer has no beginning, no ending, no being, without humility. As a ship is made for the sea, so prayer is made for humility and so humility is made for prayer."[3]

Once we have completed our instruction from Professor Failure, we are enrolled in a new course of study. We become the pupils of the professors Faith and Confidence. They turn our complete focus upon God, who becomes our confidence. We learn that God does not want merely to give us victory, but that *He is our victory.*

Often many have missed the purpose and essence of prayer. Prayer is not a time in which we come to receive something from God. Prayer is an encounter with a holy God. It is coming into His presence—entering into fellowship and a relationship with Him. It is the means by which we get to know Him. Out of the personal, intimate knowledge of God the victory of Jesus flows through us and into the world around us.

Moses was brought to this knowledge of God in the second period in his life. After He encountered God on Mount

3. Ibid., p. 23.

Horeb he was never the same. He no longer carried an ordinary rod—he carried the rod of God. He did not act with might and military strategy, but he acted with God's power and wisdom. His confidence was no longer in himself but in the God He encountered on the mountain. The victory and deliverance of the nation of Israel came as a direct result of meeting with God.

The need of every generation is men and women who pray. The most powerful resource of the church is a transformed life. The world is not attracted to Christ by fancy edifices but by men and women who have the mark of God upon their inner being.

Prayer is the branding iron of God. We will not make an impact on the world until we have been marked by the Master. The mark of God upon our inner man will bring victory to churches, communities, and nations.

We must learn that victory comes on our knees.

Prayer often avails where everything else fails. How utterly all of Monica's efforts and entreaties failed with her son! But her prayers prevailed with God, and the dissolute youth became St. Augustine, the mighty man of God. By prayer the bitterest enemies of the Gospel have become its most valiant defenders, the greatest scoundrels—the truest sons of God, and the vilest women—the purest saints! Oh, the power of prayer to reach down, down, down where hope itself seems vain, and lift men and women up, up into fellowship with and likeness to God! It is simply wonderful!

(R. A. Torrey, *How to Pray* [Moody, n.d.])

Lord, I have heard the report about Thee and I fear. O Lord, revive Thy work in the midst of the years, in the midst of the years make it known; in wrath remember mercy.

(Habakkuk 3:2)

2

The Necessity of Prayer

Throughout church history the greatest revivals have typically followed periods of spiritual darkness. During those periods small groups of people desperately desired spiritual awakening. Prayer was viewed as a *necessity* and not an *option*.

We must realize the necessity of prayer as well. There must be an outpouring of men's and women's hearts to God before there will be an outpouring of God's Spirit upon men and women. There must be a revival of praying before there can be a reaping of the harvest.

Two principles lead us to our first step toward revival. First, we must realize the desperateness of our situation. Much of the church today is backslidden. We have become subnormal in our Christian experience. We have developed a Christianity of convenience and comfort rather than character and commitment. We must recognize our need if there is to be hope for this generation.

Second, we must understand that our only hope is in God. We must thirst for communion with Jesus—a thirst that will drive us to action. We will then begin to obey God through the outpouring of our hearts to Him. Those attitudes expressed through prayer will release the power of God upon our lives, our churches, and our communities.

We will see revival in this generation only as we begin to pray.

Romania, which is experiencing a great revival, beautifully illustrates this principle. The revival is contained, however, within the northern and western portions of the country. Many of the churches in the southern and eastern parts of Romania still remain small and needy.

I was invited to preach an evangelistic crusade in a small church in the southeastern part of Romania. The people were desperate. They were greatly persecuted and few in number. Out of their desperation they began to meet together to pray. They cried unto the Lord for their communities and their friends.

I arrived in their city on a wintery Sunday evening. The church was packed. The downstairs area was filled with non-Christians. The balcony and adjoining rooms were packed with believers. I sensed the Holy Spirit's presence.

One woman brought a head supervisor from a local factory to the services. He was converted to Christ that night. Many others gave their hearts to Jesus. The next evening the supervisor's wife accepted Christ. The following evening another factory supervisor came to the services. He did not give his heart to Christ that evening, but the next day he said to the workers at the factory, "Wonderful things are happening at the church. Everyone needs to go there and hear the message!"

People stood outside in subfreezing temperatures to hear the message of Christ. Scores of people were converted. The church could not contain the crowds. It was the largest evangelical meeting in the history of that city. The Holy Spirit moved mightily in response to the desperate cry of God's people.

The Holy Spirit waits for the people of God to cry unto Him. He knows our circumstances. He is longing to deliver us. When God met Moses in the Midianite desert, He told him, "I have surely seen the affliction of My people who are in Egypt, and have given heed to their cry . . . . So I have come down to deliver them from the power of the Egyptians" (Exodus 3:7-8).

There are two conditions that must be fulfilled in order for God to deliver His people. First, we must wait for His timing. God knew the circumstances of the children of Israel. But He had promised deliverance after four hundred years of bondage (Genesis 15:13-14). God is never late and never early; He is always right on time. At the close of four hundred years He raised up a deliverer for the people.

Second, when God gets ready to move among His people, He always stirs them to cry unto Him. Although God is sovereign, He chooses to include man in His divine plan of action. Therefore, God waits for us to cry out to Him. He will even allow circumstances to enter our lives that will cause us to pray and seek Him with our whole hearts.

PRAYER AS A PRIORITY IN THE EARLY CHURCH

Jesus gave His disciples vision and passion. He also gave them an impossible task: to make disciples of all the nations. They were commissioned to win the world. But Jesus warned them, "Behold, I am sending forth the promise of My Father upon you; but you are to stay in the city until you are clothed with power from on high" (Luke 24:49).

And the disciples did stay in Jerusalem. They waited and prayed. Why did Jesus want them to remain in Jerusalem with such a great task ahead of them? There was a world that desperately needed the gospel. Why should they wait in prayer?

I believe there are three reasons that Jesus established prayer as a priority for the early church. First, their vision and passion for a lost world could only be maintained by prayer. As they spent time with the Father in prayer, they would feel what He felt and see what He saw.

Leonard Ravenhill said, "The two prerequisites to successful Christian living are vision and passion, both of which are born in and maintained by prayer. The ministry of preaching is opened to few; the ministry of prayer—the highest ministry of all human offices—is open to all."[1]

Second, not only is vision maintained by prayer, but hearts are prepared to receive the message of Christ through prayer. The gospel is eternal and spiritual in nature. Man in his natural, fallen state cannot comprehend such a message; it is foreign to his natural state of being. Therefore, we must pray that their spiritual eyes be opened.

I have seen atheists in communist countries believe in the resurrected Christ. The scales of atheism were removed from their eyes by praying saints. As a result of the moving of God's Spirit in the city in southeastern Romania, I was invited to another area of Romania. Often a pastor in Romania will be responsible for five to seven churches in different cities. A pastor begged me to preach in several cities where he ministered.

Several months later I went to minister with this pastor. The people had given themselves to weeks and months of deep, intercessory prayer. The results were phenomenal.

I preached in a small church the first Sunday morning. Approximately fifteen people were converted to Christ. The next day I preached in a nearby city. One of the deacons approached me afterward and told me he had been praying for God's wisdom and leadership. Although dangerous, he had wanted to invite one of his friends to attend the evangelistic services with him. After much prayer he decided to stop by the friend's house.

After the friend had come home from work he felt that he needed to shave and get dressed. He also felt a need to go somewhere, but he did not know where. After getting dressed he sat in his chair and waited. In a few moments the deacon from the Baptist church knocked on his door. The friend went with the deacon to the church and heard the

1. Leonard Ravenhill, *Why Revival Tarries* (Minneapolis: Bethany, 1984), p. 23.

gospel for the first time. He accepted Christ because God had prepared his heart that day.

Although unusual, that example exhibits the power of prayer to prepare people's hearts. God will not always work in the unusual ways, but we must understand the necessity of prevailing prayer. Perhaps there are no conversions in our churches because we have not seen how impossible it is for the non-Christian mind to believe. It is only when God opens their hearts to understand the message of Christ that they can accept Him. Hearts will be made receptive only as we pray.

Third, God will not only open hearts to the gospel, but He will also empower the proclaimer of the message of Christ. There is a radical difference in the pre-Pentecost and post-Pentecost lives of the disciples. Peter, the cowardly denier of Jesus, became the bold preacher of Jesus. A new sense of courage characterized the early Christians in Acts. We must realize, however, that their boldness was the fruit of their prayer lives.

PRAYER RESULTS IN SECURITY IN CHRIST

If one is to speak mightily for God, then he must walk humbly with God. Courage for Christ is a direct result of security in Christ. Prayer intensifies our fellowship with God. It is in that fellowship that the believer experiences the depth and width and height of the love of God. The Christian can face the gates of hell if he has been before the throne of heaven. Fear flees when one has basked in the perfect love of God.

The pastor in Romania again asked if I would come to another city. We couldn't believe our eyes when we arrived at the church. The city contained less than fifty evangelical Christians, but there were four times as many people gathered at the church than the building could hold.

The pastor was thrilled. He asked if I would preach outside, and I agreed. My interpreter pulled me over to the side and said, "I don't think that you understand, Sammy. It is illegal to preach outside in Romania. You could go to prison. The pastor could go to prison. Or perhaps you will be deported from the country. Your ministry will be finished in our country."

Fear filled my heart. My interpreter and I found a quiet place and prayed. We wept and confessed our fears to God. After some moments of fellowship with the Father we were secure in His love. It did not matter what our future held. We knew that God held our future.

We went back to the entrance of the church and preached. The power and glory of God were everywhere. People heard the preaching from the surrounding apartment complexes and came outside. Young people climbed into trees to listen. Others climbed on top of garages, and some listened over fences. Scores of people heard the message, and many responded.

My interpreter said that the gospel of Christ made more progress in those two nights than it had made in the past ten years. When fear and intimidation assaulted us, we needed only to run into the arms of the Father. His love made us secure. As a result the gospel went forward, and His kingdom was built.

PRAYER RESULTS IN TRANSFORMATION

The kingdom of God will grow powerfully as the people of God pray. God's kingdom has always taken its greatest steps during times of spiritual renewal and awakening. And spiritual awakening has always been ushered into the world by praying saints.

Prayer has the ability to travel across oceans and touch distant continents. Yet it is able to bring God's presence into the privacy of our own homes and hearts. Prayer can bring social justice to a nation and personal righteousness to the individual.

We will begin to experience personal victory as we enter into the private chambers of prayer. We must enter regularly and consistently. We must long for fellowship with Him. To do otherwise is rebellion. In essence it is saying, "I don't need You, Father. I can live today without Your strength and power."

E. M. Bounds stated it more forcefully when he said, "Prayer is loyalty to God. Non-praying is to reject Christ and abandon heaven. A life of prayer is the only life which heaven counts."[2]

No wonder there are so many struggling, defeated Christians today. We have abandoned the throne of heaven. We have substituted technology for "kneeology." We would rather have emotional excitement than daily fellowship with the Creator.

I once preached in a large church in Atlanta, Georgia. Although the young people there became excited about Christ, a year later I returned and discovered few were living a life of victory. No one knew why they had fallen into such a low spiritual state. Finally I asked how many of them had maintained a regular time alone with the Father in prayer. Only a couple of them said they had a consistent prayer time.

I challenged those young people to commit themselves to faithfully spend time in the Word of God and prayer. Many accepted the challenge. When I returned again a year later I found a living, dynamic group of Christian young people.

A successful youth ministry does not consist of cookies, punch, and a singing group. On the contrary, successful ministry is teaching people "to do justice, to love kindness, and to walk humbly with your God" (Micah 6:8).

We will not only secure victory for ourselves, but we can also see God transform our friends and our communities

2. E. M. Bounds, *The Reality of Prayer* (Grand Rapids: Baker, 1978), p. 35.

through prayer. The greatest work to be done for society will be the work of prayer. Nineteenth-century evangelist D. L. Moody said, "Those who have left the deepest impression on this sin cursed earth have been men and women of prayer. You will find that prayer has been the mighty power that has moved not only God, but man."[3]

Through the prayers of his wife, a former coworker of mine accepted Christ. For many months his wife was concerned about his spiritual welfare. She continually witnessed to him, but he did not respond. Finally, she *quit talking to him about God* and *started talking to God about him.* He then surrendered his life to Jesus. He has been a faithful witness and minister of the gospel ever since.

God is able to do far beyond anything that we can imagine. As much as we may love friends and family members, God loves them more. As much as we desire to help them, God can help them more. He can bring circumstances into their lives that will lead them to the cross. For the sake of our friends and family we must pray.

Non-Christians' lack of interest in spiritual matters is often a result of Christians' lack of prayer. Their unconcern may be a result of our unconcern. Why should sinners be concerned about hell when it has been years since we have wept over lost souls? Our lack of tears and lack of prayer should drive us to one conclusion: We need revival in our personal lives, our churches, and our world.

Charles Finney, the nineteenth-century revivalist and evangelist, was used of God to stir the church in America with the fires of revival. He dealt with a question that this generation also needs to seriously consider: When is there a need for revival among Christians?

His answer should stir us to prayer:

3. Quoted in Warren Wiersbe, *Classic Sermons on Prayer* (Grand Rapids: Kregel, 1987), p. 19.

1. When there is a want of brotherly love and Christian confidence among professors of religion, then there is a great need of a revival.
2. When there are dissensions, and jealousies, and evil speakings among professors of religion, then there is a great need of revival.
3. When there is a worldly spirit in the church.
4. When the church finds its members falling into gross and scandalous sins, then it is time for the church to awake and cry to God for a revival of religion.
5. When there is a spirit of controversy in the church or in the land, a revival is needful.
6. When the wicked triumph over the church, and revile them, it is time to seek for a revival of religion.
7. When sinners are careless and stupid, sinking into hell unconcerned, it is time the church should bestir itself.[4]

The twentieth-century church must confess that she stands in need of revival. Businessmen need to join together to pray. Homemakers must cry out to God for a fresh out-pouring of His Spirit. Students need to form prayer groups on campuses. We must pray!

4. V. Raymond Edman, *Finney Lives On* (Minneapolis: Bethany, 1970), pp. 89-90.

Prayer is a wonderful power placed by Almighty God in the hands of His saints, which may be used to accomplish great purposes and to achieve unusual results. Prayer reaches to everything, takes in all things great and small which are promised by God to men. The only limit to prayer are the promises of God and His ability to fulfill those promises.

(E. M. Bounds, *The Possibilities of Prayer* [Baker, 1979])

In every true prayer there are two hearts in exercise. The one is your heart, with its little, dark, human thoughts of what you need and God can do. The other is God's great heart, with its infinite, its divine purpose of blessing. What think you? To which of these two ought the larger place be given in your approach to Him? Undoubtedly, to the heart of God: everything depends upon knowing and being occupied with that. . . . This is what waiting on God is meant to teach you.

(Andrew Murray, *The Prayer Life* [Whitaker, 1981])

Faith comes from hearing, and hearing by the word of Christ.

(Romans 10:17)

3

The Possibilities of Prayer

The greatest adventure man can embark on is prayer. Prayer has the ability to take the deepest thoughts and feelings of man before the Creator. At the same time prayer brings the nature, character, and purposes of God into the heart of man. Prayer can chart and change the course of human history. It can calm the heart in the midst of a raging storm and refresh the weary saint in the battles of life.

Prayer opens the possibilities of all that heaven has to offer man. Yet this adventure into the life of prayer cannot be taken lightly. When we enter the life of prayer we walk on holy ground. We come into the presence of a living God.

Many have never entered into the life of prayer because they lack understanding of prayer's true nature. Perhaps this is why the disciples slept while Jesus prayed. And perhaps this is why the church sleeps in this generation while the world slides further and further into immorality and rebellion against God.

THE NATURE OF PRAYER

Prayer is the heart of man in communion with the heart of the Father. It is the heart of the Father bestowing grace and mercy upon the heart of man. And it is the whole heart of man seeking to know the whole heart of God. Prayer is essentially the communion of two hearts.

C. H. Spurgeon said, "True prayer is not a mere mental exercise, nor a vocal performance, but it is deeper far than that—it is spiritual communion with the Creator of heaven and earth. God is a Spirit unseen of mortal eye and only to be perceived by the inner man; our spirit within us, begotten by the Holy Ghost at our regeneration. Prayer is a spiritual business from beginning to end, and its aim and object end not with man, but reach to God Himself."[1]

This view is quite different from the modern practice of prayer. We live in an "instant" generation. We live in a technological society that can fulfill our desires immediately. We have everything from instant potatoes to instant reports on the stock market.

But there is no instant fellowship with God. We cannot rush in and out of God's presence. Prayer takes time. We must learn, as Psalm 46:10 says, to be still and know that He is God.

There are two important aspects to communion with God. First, we must understand that we only have access to communion with the Father through Jesus. Second, we must learn to wait upon the Lord and meditate on His Word.

JESUS, THE WAY INTO COMMUNION

In 1970 a spiritual awakening occurred at Asbury College and Seminary. A few weeks after the revival began I met Frank Laubach, a professor there at that time.

Along with a couple of friends, I sat at the feet of Dr. Laubach as he encouraged us from the Word of God. The elderly gentleman's words still ring in my ears: "I have been praying for years for this kind of awakening. God has answered my prayers. I am ready to go to be with Him." Then

1. Quoted in Warren Wiersbe, *Classic Sermons on Prayer* (Grand Rapids: Kregel, 1987), p. 27.

he looked directly into our eyes and said, "Young men, every morning when you awaken, take a little walk with Matthew, Mark, Luke, and John. Let them introduce you to Jesus!" Not long after our talk Dr. Laubach went to be with the Lord.

Dr. Laubach knew that only Jesus can usher us into fellowship with the Father. Without a mediator, a feeble, imperfect, sinful man would be unable to enter into the presence of a holy, almighty, all-knowing God. Paul wrote to Timothy, "For there is one God, and one mediator also between God and men, the man Christ Jesus . . . . Therefore I want the men in every place to pray, lifting up holy hands, without wrath and dissension" (1 Timothy 2:5, 8).

Jesus is our mediator because of His uniqueness. In His earthly life He was the God-man. He was the total expression of the character and heart of God in human flesh. And yet He felt the hurts, sorrows, and temptations of humanity. No one but Jesus has ever been or will ever be qualified to act as a mediator between God and man.

Jesus is the way into communion with the Father. That is why He told His disciples, "Until now you have asked for nothing in My name; ask, and you will receive, that your joy may be made full" (John 16:24). Prayer becomes an adventure because we are escorted into the presence of the Father by the Son. There is complete joy to be found in the presence of God.

Jesus is the exact representation of the nature of God. If we are to ever know intimately the heart of the Father, we must learn to look to Jesus. The purity, compassion, and wisdom of the Father are clearly understood through the Son.

WAITING ON GOD

If we are to come into the presence of God we must learn the art of waiting upon God. There is no hustle and bustle in the presence of God. David is known in Scripture as a man after God's own heart. He continually speaks in the

Psalms of waiting upon the Lord. If we are to be God's men and women we must also learn to wait upon the Lord.

Waiting upon God recognizes two important truths from Scripture: the helplessness of man and the sufficiency of Christ. As we wait upon God we understand Jesus' words, "Apart from Me you can do *nothing*" (John 15:5, emphasis added).

Andrew Murray stated, "The deep need for this waiting upon God lies equally in the nature of man and the nature of God. God, as Creator, formed man, to be a vessel in which He could show forth His power and goodness. Man was not to have in himself a fountain of life, or strength, or happiness. . . . Man was to have the joy of receiving every moment out of the fullness of God. This was his blessedness as an unfallen creature."[2]

We were created to know and love God. Without daily communion with Him it is impossible to serve Him effectively. Many Christians believe that they can work *for God* without having been *with God*. To live without waiting on the Lord is to embrace humanism and wrap it in Christian trappings. The philosophy of humanism begins with man, continues with man, and concludes with man. But Christianity begins with God. God reaches down to man, and man finds his only hope in Him. Man does not find purpose, power, and direction for his life in himself; he finds everything that He needs in God through Jesus Christ. Man must learn to live in absolute dependence upon God.

We live in a technological generation. We want quick results. As a result, many in the church have turned to the marketing industry to promote God's kingdom. The kingdom of God, however, cannot be built on slick publicity. Neither can it be built on any other form of human ingenuity. The kingdom of God will only be built by those who have the mark of the King upon their lives—the mark from having been in His presence.

2. Andrew Murray, *Waiting on God* (Chicago: Moody, n.d.), p. 16.

Many consider waiting time consuming and nonproductive. A friend once said to me, "I know a man who does not have time to develop relationships with people. He doesn't win others to Christ. He is always in his prayer closet." I thought about my friend's statement, and I realized the impossibility of it. When one has been with God, he will encounter the character and nature of God. He will encounter a God that loves man. The man or woman of prayer will be consumed by that love. The love of God will motivate the believer to action.

The man who waits upon God is not a mystic who hides from the hurts of humanity. In fact, he is quite the opposite. Those believers that have learned the art of waiting upon God have affected Christian history the most. The apostles waited on the promise of the Father, and as a result they were able to turn the Roman Empire upside down for the glory of God. Paul and four others wait upon the Lord in Acts 13, and as a result the gospel is brought to the European continent.

D. L. Moody said, "Luther and his companions were men of such mighty pleading with God, that they broke the spell of the ages, and laid nations subdued at the foot of the Cross. John Knox grasped all Scotland in his strong arms of faith; his prayers terrified tyrants. Whitefield, after much holy, faithful, closet-pleading, went to the devil's fair, and took more than a thousand souls out of the paw of the lion in one day. See a praying Wesley turn more than ten thousand souls to the Lord! Look at the praying Finney, whose prayer, faith, sermons, and writings, have shaken this whole country and sent a wave of blessing through the churches on both sides of the sea."[3]

Waiting upon God breathes fire into the souls of men. It moves men into the battle for the souls of mankind. But the man or woman of prayer does not burn out. The Christian that has learned this art of waiting will never be de-

---

3. D. L. Moody, *Prevailing Prayer* (Chicago: Moody, n.d.), p. 16.

stroyed in the battle. Isaiah 40:31 says, "Those who wait for the Lord will gain new strength; they will mount up with wings like eagles, they will run and not get tired, they will walk and not become weary."

Waiting upon God opens a new dimension to Christian living. It opens all of heaven to the believer. The Christian begins to live and walk by the Holy Spirit rather than by his own strength and power. Therefore, it is important to understand the meaning of waiting upon God.

First, one must understand what waiting does not mean. Waiting upon God is not seeking after an experience. Too many believers have made the mistake of attempting to emulate the experiences of other Christians. We read of the experiences of the great men and women of God in past years and attempt to duplicate their experiences. After hearing of a Christian friend that had an extraordinary experience with God, we may begin to seek that experience rather than God.

Early in my Christian life I read of the experiences of men such as D. L. Moody and Charles Finney. I longed to have an experience like them. I believed I would become a man of God if I could have an encounter with God like Finney and Moody had. Moody was so overwhelmed by the power of God that he had to ask God to stay His hand. And Finney said that waves and waves of liquid love flowed over him.

After I read about those experiences I told God that I was ready for His waves of love to come over me as they did Charles Finney. But they never came. I asked Him to let His power come upon me as it did upon D. L. Moody. But it never came. Finally while in prayer I discovered an insight. It was not the will of God for me to know the experience of Moody and Finney, but it was the will of God for me to know the God of Moody and Finney.

Our experiences with God are the result of the communion between God and human personalities. Although the nature of God does not change, no two personalities are the same. Finney did not have the experience of Moody, and Moody did not have the experience of Finney. But each had the mark of God upon his life.

This insight revolutionized my thinking. I learned to wait on God in order that I might know Him. I ceased striving after another person's experience. I rested in God and waited on Him. My prayer life left the realm of human striving and entered the realm of spiritual understanding.

What, then, is waiting upon God? There are three primary types of waiting upon God in Scripture. First, we wait on Jesus' second coming (1 Thessalonians 1:10). Second, we wait on God to accomplish His will, which includes waiting for instruction (Psalm 25:4-5), for answers to prayer (Luke 18:1-8), and for courage (Psalm 27:14). Many blessings and answers to prayer come after *waiting upon God over an extended period of days, months, or even years.* Third, we wait on God when we wait quietly *before Him in prayer* (Psalm 37:7). This third type of waiting is not a time for speaking to God. It is a time for listening and thinking—a time for the inner man to be quieted before God. It is a time of reflecting upon the goodness and greatness of God, of meditating on the character and the works of God.

Perhaps one of the great needs of this generation is for thinking men and women. The advent of the computer has brought artificial intelligence to the world. Many Christians have ceased to be thinkers in an age of computers and televisions. More time is spent reading the newspaper in many Christian homes than reading the Word of God. We watch murders and adultery on TV, yet we have little time to think and meditate on the splendor and glory of God.

No wonder adultery and divorce are rampant within the church. The church has become powerless to reach and transform such a needy generation. We become what we think. There is a desperate need today for creative Christian thinkers. And creative Christian thinking is a result of meditating on the biblical revelation of the Creator of the universe.

WAITING AND THE WORD OF GOD

The Word of God is the one indispensable tool for waiting on God. If we are to meditate on God's character and works, we must have a clear understanding of who He is and what He has done. If our view of God is incorrect, then we will have weak and perverted prayer lives. A thorough study of history shows that the church becomes ineffective when she forsakes Scripture. Scripture is a testimony of Jesus. Therefore it is necessary to spend time daily in the Word.

Andrew Murray stated, "Little of the Word with little prayer is death to the spiritual life. Much of the Word with little prayer gives a sickly life. Much prayer with little of the Word gives more life, but without steadfastness. A full measure of the Word and prayer each day gives a healthy and powerful life."[4]

We need to come into the presence of God with a Bible in our hands and praise in our hearts. As we wait quietly before the Lord, heaven will open. Prayer has the ability to deeply touch the soul of man. It is as timeless as eternity. Prayer reaches back into history and moves the faith of Abraham, Isaac, and Jacob into the present. It leaves its impact on future generations. It transforms tragedy into triumph. Prayer has the Word of God as its only limitation.

4. Andrew Murray, *The Prayer Life* (Springdale, Pa.: Whitaker House, 1981), p. 106.

I found I could not live without enjoying the presence of God; and if at any time a cloud came over me, I could not rest, I could not study, I could not attend to anything with the least satisfaction or benefit, until the medium was again cleared between my soul and God.
  (Charles Finney, quoted in V. Raymond Edman,
                Finney Lives On [Bethany, 1970])

Grant her honor as a fellow heir of the grace of life, so that your prayers may not be hindered.
                                    (1 Peter 3:7)

4

The Hindrances to Prayer

People often say, "Prayer is difficult for me. It seems as though my prayers only go as high as the ceiling." Sometimes that is true. Obstacles to our prayer lives really can hinder our prayers. Certain things will cause a break in our fellowship with God.

Prayer is intimacy and fellowship with God. It is that which enables us to enter into His presence. Therefore, anything that causes a break in our fellowship with God is a hindrance to prayer.

Many prayers have little or no meaning. I used to pray, "Lord, help us with this football game," or, "God, help me pass this exam." My entire concept of prayer was receiving something for myself. I believed people prayed only at church or when they were in trouble.

Much of the Christian world does not know the wonder and splendor of prayer. Why is there so little prayer in our churches today? What has happened to old-fashioned prayer meetings? Why has evangelical Christianity in the Western world lost its power in proclaiming the message of Christ?

There are numerous answers to these questions. However, one reason for the lack of spiritual power within the church is the lack of effective praying. We must remove every hindrance to prayer if we are to experience revival. The Word of God exposes obstacles to effective, powerful praying.

RELIGION WITHOUT A RELATIONSHIP WITH GOD

Religion without a relationship with God hinders us from experiencing the true meaning of prayer. Jesus said, "I am the way, and the truth, and the life; no one comes to the Father, but through Me" (John 14:6). Many churches are filled with religious people who don't have an intimate relationship with the Father. That relationship can only be secured through personal faith in Jesus Christ.

The scribes and Pharisees prayed often. Although they were religious people, they didn't have a personal relationship with God. For them, prayer was a religious duty. It was not a means of entering into the presence of the Father; it was an obligation. Without receiving Jesus as their Messiah, they would never understand the meaning of prayer.

I was a member of a church for many years, but I did not have a personal relationship with the Father through Jesus Christ. As a result, prayer was boring. It gave no meaning to my life. I tried to fill the emptiness with popularity, parties, and alcohol. But I was left empty.

Then one evening I realized that God alone is holy and perfect. I knew I was separated from Him and recognized my need for a Savior. When I invited Christ into my life, my sins were forgiven and my burden was lifted. I was escorted into the presence of the Father by His own Son.

Since that time, prayer has become one of the most exciting adventures of my life. Now I can take my Bible into the woods for an hour and experience the joy of a personal relationship with almighty God. I can have more joy in that one hour of prayer than I experienced at all the parties I attended before I became a Christian.

Only the Lamb of God can take away our sins. Only the Lamb can make us righteous and holy and provide us access to the throne of God. Without a personal knowledge of God, prayer has no real meaning.

SIN

The second hindrance to effective praying is sin. Isaiah 59:2 says, "But your iniquities have made a separation between you and your God, and your sins have hidden His face from you, so that He does not hear."

When we come into the presence of God, we will always behold one outstanding characteristic of His nature: His holiness. There is not a blemish in God; purity and impurity do not mix. If we are to have fellowship with a holy and pure God, then we must be clean before Him. David asks in Psalm 24:3-4, "Who may ascend into the hill of the Lord? And who may stand in His holy place? He who has clean hands and a pure heart, who has not lifted up his soul to falsehood, and has not sworn deceitfully." Only the pure in heart will be able to enter into God's presence.

Several years ago I was preaching an evangelistic crusade in southern Illinois. Many had been converted to Christ during the week. And God was working in the hearts of the believers as well. At the end of the week, a deacon stood and gave his testimony.

He said, "When I came to this city I was a new Christian, and I needed a job desperately. I applied for the job that I now have. It was stated on the application form that any falsification of information would result in an automatic dismissal from the job. I lied about some of my qualifications. But it was never discovered.

"However, every time that I would try to pray, it seemed impossible. God would remind me of how I had lied on my application. Consequently, I spent little time in prayer."

With tears streaming down his face he said, "This week I decided that my fellowship with the heavenly Father was more important than the security of my job. I confessed to my supervisors what I had done. They have forgiven me and will allow me to continue my work. But praise the Lord! I now have sweet communion with the Father. I can come before Him with a clean conscience. Prayer has again become a vital part of my Christian life."

We must learn that prayer is communion with the Father. And if we are to commune with Him, we must have clean hands and a pure heart. God can only be seen through the eyes of a pure heart.

PRIDE

The third obstacle to effective praying is pride. James 4:6 says, "God is opposed to the proud, but gives grace to the humble." A thorough study of what the Bible says about pride reveals that God not only hates pride, but He promises destruction for the proud in heart (Proverbs 16:18-19).

If God is opposed to what is in our hearts, then we can never develop intimacy with Him. In Luke 18:9-14 Jesus tells a parable of two men who went to pray. God honored the prayer of one of the men, but He would have nothing to do with the prayer of the other man.

One prayed to *himself*. He was a proud, religious man. He was not like others who committed adultery and cheated people out of their money. He tried to tell God how great he was. But God had nothing to do with this man. This man trusted in himself and prayed to himself, and his prayers only reached the ceiling.

The other man was different. He was broken over his sinful condition. He beat his breast and wept as he said, "God, be merciful to me, the sinner!" God heard this man's prayer and answered it. Jesus concludes the parable in verse 14 by saying, "For everyone who exalts himself shall be humbled, but he who humbles himself shall be exalted." God honors the prayer spoken from a heart of humility.

Pride compares us to others to find someone that has not lived up to our standards. But humility does not look upon men. It looks only upon God. Therefore a praying heart will always be a humble heart. There is no room in the inner chamber of prayer for pride.

BROKEN RELATIONSHIPS

Another reason for ineffective prayer is a broken relationship. First Peter 3:7 says, "You husbands likewise, live with your wives in an understanding way . . . and grant her honor as a fellow heir of the grace of life, so that your prayers may not be hindered."

Many view prayer as an escape from everyday living. They believe prayer is mystical and of no practical value. They see no relationship between prayer and interpersonal relationships.

True prayer, however, draws our attention to the nature and character of God. We become like Him as we recognize His attributes. When we emerge from the inner chamber of prayer we will love with a revolutionary love—the love of the Father. Our capacity to love will be broadened and deepened.

Consequently, prayer and interpersonal relationships are interwoven. Prayer affects our relationships, and our relationships affect our ability to pray. Many times I have needed to ask my wife and my children to forgive me. I could not be in harmony with God when I was out of tune with my family.

My wife and I have attempted to build our marriage on biblical principles. This means we decided never to go to sleep with a breach between us. One evening several years ago, however, we had a disagreement that we did not resolve. I cannot recall what the disagreement was, but I remember believing that my wife was in the wrong.

When we went to bed that evening my wife went to sleep quickly and soundly, but I tossed and turned. The Holy Spirit was convicting me of my wrong attitude. I tried to argue. I prayed, "God, I'm right! She's wrong! Why does she have peace, and I feel Your conviction?"

As I struggled in misery, I realized that I could not be in fellowship with God and out of fellowship with my wife. I asked her forgiveness, and peace was restored. If we are to be effective in prayer, we must mend broken relationships. We cannot have fellowship with God without restored relationships with our brothers and sisters in Christ.

BUSYNESS

The fifth hindrance to prayer is busyness. Paul writes in Ephesians 5:16, "Making the most of your time, because the days are evil."

We live in one of the most exciting generations. There are more people living today than in any previous generation. The opportunities to impact our world for Christ have never been greater. We have the resources. But there is one disturbing question. Where are the workers? There is a ripe harvest, but there is a shortage of workers.

Jesus said that the solution to the problem of workers is found in prayer (Matthew 9:37-38). But that presents another problem. Where are the men and women of prayer?

Too many of us have become so busy that we have little time for God. Our lives have become obsessed with climbing the ladder of success and resting in the easy chair of entertainment. A prayerless church exists in this generation. We cannot get people to prayer meetings, but we have no problem amassing large crowds for Christian entertainment. Our church schedules are filled with events oriented toward entertainment, and we have no time left to seek God. We have become like the Laodicean church. Jesus is on the outside knocking, wanting to come in and have fellowship with us.

A. W. Tozer said, "For centuries the Church stood solidly against every form of worldly entertainment, recognizing it for what it was—a device for wasting time, a refuge from the disturbing voice of conscience, a scheme to divert attention from moral accountability. For this she got herself abused roundly by the sons of this world. But of late she has become tired of the abuse and has given over the struggle. She appears to have decided that if she cannot conquer the great god, Entertainment, she may as well join forces with him and make what use she can of his powers."[1]

In a radio interview I was asked to describe the difference between a typical church in the West and a typical church in Romania. The answer was simple. The difference lies in what it takes to get a crowd. In the West we can get a crowd to a Christian concert, a Christian aerobic class, or a church social. But the prayer meeting is empty.

In Romania there are no Christian concerts. Christians do not get together for exercise. There are no church socials. But the prayer meeting is full. They do not have a schedule that has left Jesus on the outside. A schedule that is too busy for God is too busy. The need exists for men and women who mean business with God, who will give God priority in their lives, schedules, and churches.

SELFISHNESS

The final impediment to prayer is selfishness. James 4:3 says, "You ask and do not receive, because you ask with wrong motives, so that you may spend it on your pleasures." Prayer is a time of submitting our lives to the lordship of Christ. How then can we bring our own selfish desires and activities to God's throne and expect His blessing?

One of our greatest problems is that we have a generation of self-seeking, manipulative Christians. We have learned the methods of the world and tried to mingle them with the method of God. Many well-meaning believers initiate an idea or ministry without consulting the Father. Mass-marketing techniques and appeals for funds are used to

---

1. A. W. Tozer, *The Root of the Righteous* (Harrisburg, Pa.: Christian Publications, 1955), pp. 32-34.

launch ministries. Things often go well until we reach the limits of human ability. Then we begin to pray fervently for God's assistance.

But God refuses to answer. He had nothing to do with self-motivated and self-initiated prayer in the beginning, and He has nothing to do with it now. The windows of heaven are open only to prayer that is initiated and centered in the will of God rather than the will of man.

A. W. Tozer calls us to search our hearts and our motives: "It is only when we introduce our own will into our relation to God that we get into trouble. When we weave into the pattern of our lives threads of our own selfish desires we instantly become subject to hindrances from the outside. If I mingle some pet religious enterprise of mine with the will of God and come to think of them as one, I can be hindered in my religious life."[2]

Jesus is our model in prayer. He made a remarkable statement that provides insight into the reason for His powerful prayer life. He said, "I can do nothing on My own initiative. As I hear, I judge; and My judgment is just, because I do not seek My own will, but the will of Him who sent Me" (John 5:30). Jesus never worked a miracle in His own power or performed a ministry out of His own desire. He only did the will of the Father. He understood the art of objective listening, so that when the Father spoke, He acted.

To Jesus, prayer was not giving the Father a list of the things He wanted. Prayer was quietly listening to the command of the Father. Jesus then believed and trusted in the Father to give Him the power and resources to accomplish His will. As a result, all of heaven was released. The lame walked. The blind could see. The dead were raised. The captives were set free. The Son was in harmony with the Father.

Let us put aside every obstacle that would keep us from that same harmony with the Father. There are nations to be

2. Ibid., p. 130.

captured for Christ. There are souls to be saved and hearts to be healed. We must not allow this generation to slip further toward hell. Let us say with the author of Hebrews, "Let us also lay aside every encumbrance, and the sin which so easily entangles us, and let us run with endurance the race that is set before us, *fixing our eyes on Jesus,* the author and perfecter of faith" (Hebrews 12:1-2, emphasis added).

God wants consecrated men because He wants praying men. Consecration and prayer meet in the same man. Prayer is the tool with which the consecrated man works. Consecrated men are agents through whom prayer works. Prayer helps the consecrated man in maintaining his attitude of consecration, keeps him alive to God, and aids him doing the work to which he is called and to which he has given himself. Consecration enables one to get the most out of his praying.

(E. M. Bounds, *The Essentials of Prayer*
[Baker, 1987])

Blessed are the pure in heart, for they shall see God.
(Matthew 5:8)

5

The Life That Prays

Years ago as I was traveling in an Eastern European country I met an elderly man who had spent several years in prison for his faith. After being released from prison, his life was continually in danger because of his ministry. Although he constantly faced the threat of death, his life remained pure and loyal to Jesus.

He was a man who understood the nature of prayer. When he went to prison, he knew that although his sons were top students in their schools, they would not be allowed to study in universities. Upon graduation from high school, his oldest son went to work in a factory.

His father prayed from his prison cell. One day the head of the communist party in the factory said to his son, "You have potential. You would be of more benefit to our nation if you studied in the university. I am going to recommend that you be allowed to study there."

The son not only studied in a university, but he studied in one of the outstanding universities in the world. He is presently one of the leading scholars in that nation and a committed Christian. Through the years that father prayed every one of his sons into the university.

I wondered how this man's prayers could change the decisions of government leaders. He said with tears running down his face, "Many people come to my country and want to make a big fire for God. I do not want to make a big fire for God. I want to be consumed by God's fire until I am ashes. When I am ashes, then I will see the glory of God."

He said to me, "When I am consumed totally by God's fire, then I will see His glory. Do you understand?"

I wanted to say that I understood. But I knew that the man understood the holiness of God in a way that I did not. He experienced a depth in his prayer life that I desired. My encounter with this godly man opened my eyes to a tremendous truth about prayer: *Holiness of heart and power in prayer are inseparable.* A life that prays is a life that is wholly yielded to the will of God. It is a life that recognizes the majesty of God and has submitted to His kingship. It is a life that has power and authority in prayer.

TRUE PRAYER PRODUCES HOLINESS OF HEART

True prayer will always produce holy living. And holy living produces powerful praying. One might wonder which comes first—holiness of heart or power in prayer. I believe that the answer is simple: neither and both.

Powerful praying and holiness of heart are not achieved by human efforts. They transpire when one encounters a holy God. Study the great men of faith. They became great only by the sovereign grace of God. God sought them, and when they encountered His holiness they would never be the same.

Moses was such a man. When he encountered God he was in the Midianite desert. A sense of failure haunted him. He wanted to help his people, but he felt helpless.

He was not seeking God while he was shepherding his flock on Mount Horeb. But God was seeking Moses. Moses saw an ordinary bush that was made extraordinary by the fire of God. Although the bush was burning, it was not destroyed. When God had the attention of Moses, He called him by name. God told Moses to take off his shoes because he was standing on holy ground.

Only Moses' sandals were between his feet and holy ground. In the same way, many times it is only the small things in our lives that keep us from coming into the presence of a holy God. We must remove anything from our lives that keeps us from planting our lives in the holiness of God.

The grace of God is magnificent! And He is not far off. Andrew Murray stated, "Someone has said that the holiness of God is the expression of the unspeakable distance by which He in His righteousness is separated from us, and yet also of the inseparable nearness in which He in His love longs to hold fellowship with us and dwell in us."[1]

When we encounter a holy God we must bow before Him. His fire will consume the sin that stains our hearts and separates us from Him. Our hearts will no longer belong to the world; they will belong to God. It is impossible to hold onto a holy God with one hand and the world with the other. When we let go of the world and cling to God with both hands, we will not only be on holy ground, but we will be on praying ground.

Moses' life would never be the same after His encounter with God. His heart was set apart for God's divine purpose. He became known as the friend of God. Exodus 33:11 says, "The Lord used to speak to Moses face to face, just as a man speaks to his friend."

Too few people are known as the friends of God. Many are known as great communicators and ministers, great musicians and workers. But a great need exists for friends of God.

A friend of God will have the imprint of holiness on his heart and the tool of prayer in his hand. He will live every day with a separated and seeking heart. Many claim to have a seeking heart without having a separated heart. They claim to pray and seek God but continue to live with sin

1. Andrew Murray, *The Prayer Life* (Springdale, Pa.: Whitaker House, 1981), p. 75.

tucked away. They may fool others and may even deceive themselves, but they will never fool God. Only a holy heart will be honored in the presence of a holy God.

True Prayer Seeks God

Prayer is not merely a religious exercise that Christians perform. Neither is it seeking a handout from God. Prayer is seeking to know God. It is seeking Him with our whole hearts.

The Old Testament prophet Jeremiah sent a letter to the priests, the prophets, and the people Nebuchadnezzar had taken into exile in Babylon. In that letter he stated the kind of prayer that God acknowledges. "Then you will call upon Me and come and pray to Me, and I will listen to you. And you will seek Me and find Me, when you search for Me with all your heart. And I will be found by you" (Jeremiah 29:12-14).

When a person searches for God with his whole heart, only then is God found. The heart of man is the central core of a person—the inner man. The Greek word for heart is *kardia,* which means, "the chief organ of physical life." W. E. Vine said that the heart "occupies the most important place in the human system. By an easy transition, the word came to stand for man's entire mental and moral activity, both the rational and the emotional elements. In other words, the heart is used figuratively for the hidden springs of the personal life. . . . The heart, in its moral significance in the Old Testament, includes the emotions, the reason, and the will."[2]

The heart can experience both the emotion of joy (Proverbs 15:13, 15) and anxiety (Proverbs 12:25). It has the ability to understand (1 Kings 3:9) and think (Luke 2:19). It can exercise the will (Ephesians 6:6). Therefore, one must pray with his intellect, emotions, and will if he is to find God.

2. W. E. Vine, *Vine's Expository Dictionary of New Testament Words* (McLean, Va.: MacDonald, n.d.), pp. 546-47.

TRUE PRAYER PURSUES THE WILL OF GOD

Prayer is a priority in the lives of many Romanian Christians. Many of them have learned to pray with their whole hearts. I have met young men and women who diligently search Scripture in order to understand God fully. I have learned never to ask them what verse of Scripture they are memorizing; it is more appropriate to ask what chapter or what book of the Bible they are memorizing.

A young Romanian singing group traveled with me as I preached in evangelistic campaigns. In order to be a part of the singing group, the singers had to memorize 1 John, James, and 1 Peter. When they sang, they would quote a chapter of Scripture between songs. They would continue in this manner throughout their musical program.

The most powerful, praying Christians that I have met are some of those Christians in Romania. They understand the nature and the character of God because they have filled their minds with Scripture.

It is inspiring to go to a prayer meeting in Romania. Not only do many pray with an understanding of the Word of God, but many are free to pray with their emotions. They weep when they pray for non-Christians. They rejoice when they thank God for the good things He has done.

But there is one outstanding characteristic of those Christians that has challenged my prayer life. They pray with a heart that is set on doing the will of God. Although the will of God often brings suffering and persecution into their lives, they pray with a will that is bent toward God. They have learned to search for God with their whole hearts.

Most Christians in the Western world pray with only part of their hearts. Although many have a good knowledge of the Bible and the attributes of God, they pray with only their minds. We must learn to weep as Jesus wept over a lost humanity. We must learn to hurt as Jesus hurts for the non-

Christian world. We must not fear praying with our emotions.

I am not referring to emotionalism; I am referring to praying with the passion of Christ. It is biblical to weep for souls. Perhaps we have lost our ability to weep for the lost. Perhaps our hearts have been far from the heart of God.

On the other hand, there are Christians that pray only with their emotions. Their prayers are rooted in experience and feelings. Many love to have a mystic feeling but have little understanding of the attributes and nature of God. Christians must learn to pray according to sound biblical principles. Effective praying will always be rooted in the truth of God's Word. Effective praying will not be given to emotional tangents and experiences. Experience and emotion will always come under the searchlight of God's Word. They must live up to the truth. However, there is one element of prayer that has been lost by many Christians today: *the will.*

Perhaps the deepest and most powerful moment in the prayer life of Jesus took place on the Mount of Olives. Jesus was about to face death. He knew He would have to face the sins of people from every generation. Under those circumstances He prayed, "My Father, if it is possible, let this cup pass from Me; yet not as I will, but as Thou wilt" (Matthew 26:39).

The man who is broken and bent in his will becomes mighty with God. The man who searches for God with his whole heart (mind, will, and emotions) will find God. And the man who finds God will have a keen sense of God's purpose. That person will be on a mission from God. That person's life will move people because it has been transformed.

To pray with a will surrendered to God is to risk our lives for God. Too many in this generation seek comfortableness. Too many use prayer as an escape from what is difficult.

Often prayer and suffering go hand in hand. Suffering ushers us into a new realm of dependence upon God. In our sufferings we experience His sufficiency.

Prayer can accomplish four major tasks in suffering. First, prayer delivers us *from* that which we suffer. God will on occasion work a mighty victory in our lives. We find freedom from our suffering by the power of God obtained in prayer. Second, prayer delivers the grace of God to us in our suffering. That grace enables us to endure the suffering. Third, prayer delivers us into the hands of God's comfort. Jesus said, "Blessed are those who mourn, for they shall be comforted" (Matthew 5:4). Finally, prayer delivers the character of God into our lives when we suffer.

Jesus came to the hurting and the afflicted. The only true source of godly character comes from being in His presence. In those times of need, He meets with us.

Our problems need to be dealt with in the light of God's eternal purpose. When Jesus prayed in the Garden, He was not looking for a temporary reprieve from His pending problem. He prayed for God's eternal purpose and will. That kind of prayer is powerful. E. M. Bounds said, "Prayer is no little thing. It does not concern the petty interests of one person. The littlest prayer broadens out by the will of God till it touches all worlds, conserves all interests, and enhances man's greatest wealth, and God's greatest good."[3]

True prayer, then, is submission to the will of God. One cannot effectively enter into the secret chamber of prayer with any strings attached to his own will. The true man or woman of prayer will enter that chamber with the words of Jesus, "Not as I will, but as Thou wilt" (Matthew 26:39). Comfort is not the issue to the person of prayer. The man or woman of prayer has set his or her sights on the eternal purpose of God. That life will be a holy life. It will be a life given to prayer.

3. E. M. Bounds, *The Reality of Prayer* (Grand Rapids: Baker, 1980), p. 13.

Part 2

Instruction for Prayer

Lord, teach us to pray. (Luke 11:1)

Prayer, praise and thanksgiving all go in company. A close relationship exists between them. Praise and thanksgiving are so near alike that it is not easy to distinguish between them or define them separately.

(E. M. Bounds, *The Essentials of Prayer* [Baker, 1987])

Therefore do not be like them; for your Father knows what you need, before you ask Him. Pray, then, in this way: "Our Father who art in heaven, hallowed by Thy name."

(Matthew 6:8-9)

6

Praise: A Response to the Greatness and Goodness of God

The greatest discovery that a person can make is found in a knowledge of why he was created. In the same way, the greatest tragedy in life is for one to live without knowing why he was created. Value and worth are directly related to purpose. A car that does not transport is worth little because it does not do that for which it was created. A pen that does not write is useless because it does not accomplish its purpose. A person that does not fulfill what he was created for is the most miserable of all people.

Basically there are three types of people. First, there are people who have no purpose in life. They drift aimlessly through life. They go to school, get a job, find a spouse, work, raise a family, retire, and eventually die. They do not really live; they simply exist. The most miserable of all people in life are people without a purpose.

The second type is people with a wrong purpose. They are the superachievers who climb the ladders of financial, political, social, or religious success. They have a purpose, but their purpose is directly related to their performance. The more they achieve, the better they feel about themselves. They put their ladder in life against a wall and climb as high and as fast as they can.

But they end up frustrated in life. They climb their ladders only to discover that they have put them against the wrong walls. They are the most likely to burn out or experience the greatest trauma in mid-life. One day they awaken to discover that they have been pursuing the wrong purpose in life. They become disillusioned.

The third type of person is the most joyful and fulfilled. He is the person that has found the right purpose in life. He knows why he was created, and he has given his life to that purpose. There is no greater joy in life than to fulfill God's purpose and plan.

JESUS' TEACHING ON PRAYER

Jesus fulfilled His purpose in His earthly life from His birth until His dying breath. His entire earthly life was fulfilling that for which He was sent.

A person who lives in the center of the will of God will always disturb those outside of God's will and purpose. An expert in Mosaic law was greatly disturbed by the life of Jesus. He tested Him with the question, "Teacher, which is the great commandment in the Law?" (Matthew 22:36). When Jesus answered the lawyer, He gave us a summation of God's purpose and plan for man. He said, "You shall love the Lord your God with all your heart, and with all your soul, and with all your mind. This is the great and foremost commandment" (vv. 37-38).

Jesus continued, "A second is like it, 'You shall love your neighbor as yourself'" (v. 39). Then Jesus made a phenomenal statement. He said, "On these two commandments depend the whole Law and the Prophets" (v. 40). Jesus tells us that the law and the prophets were Holy Spirit-breathed to teach us how to live. If we are to live in fulfillment of God's purpose, then we must do two things. We must love God, and we must be an expression of His love to our fellowman.

Man was created to know and love God intimately. It is unreasonable to believe that we can love God with our whole hearts without a personal, intimate knowledge of Him. And we will never come to know Him intimately without spending personal time with Him.

Purpose in life always dictates priorities in life. We make time for things that are important to us. We have a time to get up, go to work, eat, and go to sleep. The man that has no time for prayer is the one who says with his life that knowing God is not really all that important. He can even be busy with religious activities and miss God's purpose for his life.

Jesus' disciples recognized the quality of His life and wanted to learn from Him. They ate with Him, walked with Him, and listened intently to His teaching.

But there was one aspect of His life that especially challenged them. They said, "Lord, teach us to pray" (Luke 11:1). They did not ask Jesus to teach them to preach, work miracles, or heal the sick. They wanted to know how to pray. They saw the revolutionary purpose of Jesus' life. And that life demanded the priority of prayer. Therefore, they wanted to know how to make prayer a priority in their lives.

Jesus restated to them what He had taught on the mountain. In Matthew 5-7 Jesus explains the nature of His kingdom. And He gave great priority to teaching the multitudes the importance of prayer.

Just as purpose dictates priorities in life, priorities always produce a plan to fulfill our purpose. Jesus gave His disciples a plan through which they could love God and become an expression of His love to their fellowmen. The method of Jesus for discipleship was to teach men and women to pray. Prayer would usher them into a loving, intimate relationship with the Father.

Jesus taught His disciples the principle of intimacy in prayer. He said, "When you pray, you are not to be as the hypocrites; for they love to stand and pray in the synagogues and on the street corners, in order to be seen by men. Truly I say to you, they have their reward in full. But you, when you pray, go into your inner room, and when you have shut the door, pray to your Father who is in secret, and your Father who sees in secret will repay you" (Matthew 6:5-6).

The purpose of prayer is not the applause of men. The purpose of prayer is intimacy with the Father. Men and women who have made the greatest impact on the world for the glory of God have had an intimate, private relationship with the Father. They have discovered that the power of public ministry comes from the private chambers of prayer.

There is no room for backslapping, ego building, or reputation seeking in the prayer closet. There is only room for a heart that eagerly pursues God.

A study of the men of God of past centuries clearly displays this principle. It has been said of Hudson Taylor that the sun did not rise in China without finding Taylor in his private place of prayer. Taylor founded the China Inland Mission and was mightily used of God to impact that country for Christ.

A. W. Tozer pastored a church in Chicago for many years. One time after a minister arrived in Chicago, Tozer called him and said, "This city is a devil's den. It is a very difficult place to minister the Word of God, and you will come up against much opposition from the enemy. If you ever want to pray with me, I'm at the lakeside every morning at five-thirty. Just make your way down and we can pray together." One day the minister was troubled and about six o'clock he went to the lakeside. He found A. W. Tozer prostrate in the sand worshiping God.[1] Tozer was a prophetic voice to the church of the twentieth century, and his message grew out of private intimacy with God.

1. Joseph S. Carroll, *How to Worship Jesus Christ* (Memphis: Riverside Press, 1984), p. 4.

Intimacy with God will always be found in a fresh, living relationship with the Father. That relationship necessitates that we have a time and place to regularly and consistently meet with Him.

When we come into God's presence we must approach Him with genuineness and sincerity. We must never attempt to impress God with our spirituality and religiosity. Jesus taught His disciples to be careful about how they approached the throne of heaven. He said, "When you are praying, do not use meaningless repetition, as the Gentiles do, for they suppose that they will be heard for their many words" (Matthew 6:7). God is not impressed with the loudness or softness of our voices. He is not impressed with the beauty or multiplicity of our words. He is impressed with the sincerity of our hearts.

Approaching the Throne of God

After we have sincerity of heart, we are prepared to approach the throne of God. We must then return to the statement of the disciples, "Lord, teach us to pray" (Luke 11:1). How do we pray? Are there biblical guidelines for prayer?

There are no better principles of prayer than those Jesus gives in Matthew 6:9-13. Many Christians have recited these principles numerous times in church services. Few have learned, however, to enter into an intimate fellowship with the Father through these principles. I believe that not only are the principles stated in Matthew 6:9-13 important, but the order in which they are stated is also significant.

Jesus opened the door to the life of prayer with praise: "Our Father who art in heaven, hallowed be Thy name. Thy kingdom come. Thy will be done" (vv. 9-10). And He closed the door to prayer with worship: "For Thine is the kingdom, and the power, and the glory, forever. Amen" (v. 13). We both enter our secret chamber of prayer with our focus on God and leave the prayer closet with our focus on God. All of the requests between entering and exiting are a response to God's nature and character.

Too much of prayer is shallow and superficial. It begins and ends with the needs of people, reducing God to a heavenly Santa Claus. Much prayer is simply, "I need this," and, "Give me that."

Jesus taught us to open the door of prayer with praise and thanksgiving. Praise is a response to the greatness of God, and thanksgiving is a response to the goodness of God. Praise acknowledges the attributes of God, whereas thanksgiving acknowledges the deeds of God. The psalmist said, "Let us come before His presence with thanksgiving" (Psalm 95:2).

One of the attributes of Jesus mentioned in Revelation 5:5 is that He is the "Lion that is from the tribe of Judah." The Lion is a representation of the kingship of Jesus. And the name *Judah* means "praise." Jesus is the King from the tribe of praise. We need to enter into the presence of the Father by beholding the King with praise.

Many Christians have complained that their prayer lives have become too ritualistic. They have no joy in prayer. Perhaps this is because they have reduced prayer to focusing on their needs rather than focusing on the character, attributes, and deeds of God. The great saints of old used two tools for their prayer lives: a Bible and a hymnbook. The Bible gave them an explanation of the attributes of God, and the hymnbook gave them an expression of love for the attributes and deeds of God.

The church would benefit from Christians bringing these tools to their prayer chambers. We need to learn to praise and give thanks to the Father with simple and sincere devotion. In the presence of God there are joy and reverence.

Prayer also brings us into another dimension—the dimension of the heavenly. When we enter the dimension of the heavenly we discover the magnificence of the character of God. When our sight is fully set on Him, we will see Him for who He is.

"OUR FATHER"

God is "our Father" (Matthew 6:9). Jesus taught His disciples to enter the presence of God with the understanding that He is our loving, tender Father. John MacArthur says in his exposition of Matthew 6:9, "The Aramaic term Jesus uses in Matthew 6:9 is *Abba*. That is an intimate, warm, familial term. God is not a distant ogre or a capricious, immoral Being who steps on His subjects. He is a loving, tender, caring Father. . . . All prayer begins with the recognition that God is a loving Father."[2]

The Fatherhood of God was at the core of the teaching and prayer life of Jesus. In His own prayers Jesus continually referred to God as Father. The most in-depth look at the prayer life of Jesus is found in John 17. Jesus' first word in that prayer is "Father." In Matthew 7:7-11 Jesus teaches the multitudes to ask, seek, and knock. He taught them that there is a loving Father that is eagerly waiting to meet them at their point of need.

This poses a problem for many people in this generation. Because there has been so much abuse of children by fathers, the term *father* can have a negative, perverted connotation for some believers. Jesus teaches, however, that the nature of our Father is *goodness*. He is a good Father, perfect in His goodness. He said, "If you then, being evil, know how to give good gifts to your children, how much more shall your *Father* who is in heaven give what is *good* to those who ask Him!" (Matthew 7:11, emphasis added).

Everything about the Father is good. It is in His nature to do good to His children. When we focus on the goodness of the Father, it makes miraculous changes in our attitudes toward life. Upon graduation from high school, someone said to me, "Young man, it is time for you to face the hard, cruel world." Since that time I have discovered that the world *can* be hard and cruel. It is easy to become a negative, cynical person in such a world. But when one focuses daily

2. John MacArthur, *The Disciples' Prayer* (Chicago: Moody, 1986), p. 36.

on the perfect goodness of the heavenly Father, his entire perspective changes. He is infected with a positive, loving attitude that flows from a positive, loving Father.

On one occasion when my family was traveling with me in Romania, my wife, Tex, and my daughter, Renée, were scheduled to meet my son, Dave, and me at a certain place at noon. When Dave and I arrived, we saw a crowd of around two hundred people in the middle of the street approximately one hundred meters from where we had parked our automobile. A young man from the church came running toward us and screamed frantically, "Sammy, Sammy, it's Renée!"

We ran to the crowd. We found Tex bent over ten-year-old Renée, trying to comfort her. She had been hit by a car. I helped put her on a stretcher and into an ambulance. As I rode with her in the ambulance, Renée cried and said, "Daddy, I don't want to die. I don't want to die. I want to live. I want to live and come back to sing for Jesus in Romania."

I fought back tears as I tried to tell Renée that she would be OK. At the hospital doctors ran tests to determine the extent of the injuries. The initial prognosis was not good.

Tex was detained by the police. The policeman on duty kept her passport and confiscated our automobile, although it had nothing to do with the accident. About two hours later my wife and our team finally arrived at the hospital.

Tex and I left Collynn Wood, one of our team members, with Renée while we returned to the site of the accident. I thought that the policeman would be understanding if I spoke to him. Instead, he refused to give Tex's passport back to her and threatened both of us with six months in prison because Renée had crossed the street alone. After our meeting with him, I returned to our hotel and quickly changed clothes. I dropped off Tex at the hospital and drove to the church where I was scheduled to speak.

My mind was in confusion. I had come to this communist country to preach the gospel, with a heart to serve God, but it seemed as if everything that was dear to me was being destroyed. I could not understand it. As I sat in the pastor's office two Romanian friends came in and said, "Sammy, it's time to go preach." The crowds were waiting for me. I looked at them with tears in my eyes and said, "I can't preach. I just can't do it. I'm sorry." They left the room, found a quiet place, and began to pray for me.

In that empty room I felt defeated. I felt as though I could not pray. Then I remembered the words of Jesus, "Our Father." I began to meditate on the Fatherhood of God. I remembered the great deeds that He had done—they were all good. And as I focused on the goodness of the Father, a peace that defied human understanding enveloped me.

I was able to preach, and many were converted to Christ. After praying at the close of the invitation, I opened my eyes to find a note from Tex on the pulpit. It said, "Renée is OK. She has been released from the hospital. We are at the hotel. I love you. Tex." Praise to the Father swelled in my heart. When I returned to the hotel, I found that Tex's passport had been returned, and our automobile had been released.

The goodness of God does not ignore trouble and problems in life; it brings victory and peace to our lives in the midst of trouble. The psalmist writes in Psalm 107:1, "Oh give thanks to the Lord, for He is good." Throughout the psalm the psalmist speaks of the problems and difficulties in life. Then he tells of how good God is in the midst of those difficulties. We can never fully appreciate the nature and attributes of the Father until we rest in the assurance that He is perfect in His goodness. God is so good!

Even when bad things touch our lives, we only have to look to the Father. He is good. He can even cause bad things to work together for good to those who love Him. When the

Father touches the bad situations of our lives, He supernaturally causes good to come forth from those situations. He is a good Father.

The enemy will accuse God at this point. He will come to us and show us the evil in the world. He vividly describes the atrocities throughout history. And he says that God is the cause and source of evil. The moment that we begin to entertain that thought, we lose power in prayer. The Father longs to express His goodness to His children. If we are to be powerful in prayer, we must have a clear view of His goodness.

Jesus taught His disciples to pray "Our Father." The Fatherhood of God expresses the nearness and tenderness of God. God knows and is concerned about the details of our lives.

"WHO ART IN HEAVEN"

Jesus also taught His disciples to pray, "Who art in heaven." Although "our Father" places the focus of prayer on the closeness of God, "who art in heaven" focuses on how far above man God dwells. God is no mere man. He is the Creator of the universe. He alone sits supremely on the throne of heaven. A believer is never to enter into prayer disrespectfully. He must acknowledge the supreme, divine nature of the One he approaches.

The phrase "who art in heaven" focuses our attention on four attributes of God: the omnipresence of God, the omnipotence of God, the omniscience of God, and the eternal nature of God. Prayer moves us from the earthly to the heavenly. Praise flows from the heart of the man or woman who takes time to acknowledge the greatness of God.

The omnipresence of God is an attribute of God that is foundational for the man or woman of prayer. God is everywhere. He is on His throne in heaven and yet near to man on earth. There is no place in the universe where God does not dwell.

Canon W. G. H. Holmes of India said that he once saw Hindu worshipers tapping on trees and stones and whispering, "Are you there? Are you there?"[3] They were seeking to find a god dwelling in one of those places. The follower of Jesus, however, does not need to search for the dwelling place of God. He can climb the highest mountain and meet God. He can go to the deepest ocean and encounter God. No place on earth or in heaven exists without the presence of God. This truth broadens the prayer life to the most unusual places. That is why the apostle Paul could encounter the living God in a Philippian jail cell two thousand years ago. That is why today's disciples can meet God at any place, in any country, on any continent. God is there.

The omnipresence of God not only gives the man or woman of prayer access to God in any place, but it also gives him or her the ability to pray for people everywhere. This attribute of God is the foundational characteristic that opens the door for intercessory prayer. One of the greatest problems of prayer in this generation is limited vision among God's people. Too many people pray in the context of their own little world. They become entrapped by tunnel vision. Because God is everywhere His concerns are global. As we focus on the omnipresence of God, our prayer concerns will broaden to every corner of the earth.

Not only is God everywhere, but He is there all of the time. He is eternal in nature. He was before the beginning and will be after the end. Too many Christians pray only with a view of the here and now. When we enter into the presence of God, however, we are leaving the realm of the temporal and entering the realm of the eternal. Prayer has the power to clear the slate of yesterday and paint the picture of life for tomorrow.

We can stand on the promise of Abraham, Isaac, and Jacob while we trust God to shape our future. When Moses

3. A. W. Tozer, *The Knowledge of the Holy* (New York: Harper & Row, 1961), pp. 75-76.

encountered God, he asked Him about His name. God said that His name is "I AM WHO I AM" (Exodus 3:14). He told Moses to tell the children of Israel that "I AM" had sent him.

It is amazing that thousands of years later God still remains "I AM." He does not grow old. The God of the men and women of faith in the past centuries is our God today. He is ready to work in this generation as much as He did with Abraham, Isaac, and Jacob. When we enter our prayer chamber, we need to focus on the eternal nature of God.

Because God is everywhere, all of the time, it is then possible to understand that He is omniscient. He knows everything. This attribute of God makes prayer exciting. He not only knows every detail of our lives, but He knows the deep hurts and needs of the billions of inhabitants on this earth. As we focus on God and His omniscience, we can pray with a new confidence. When we do not understand life's circumstances, we can rest assured that He does. That is why Proverbs 1:7 says, "The fear of the Lord is the beginning of knowledge."

God knows everything, but we only know and understand in part. But when we focus on the omniscience of God and revere Him, we then begin to know and understand life. We will be able to pray effectively when we recognize that only He knows and understands everything.

God not only knows everything all of the time, in every place, but He also is all-powerful. He is omnipotent and sovereign. When Jesus was placed in a tomb after His death, the demons wanted to keep Him there. But the Father raised the Son from the dead. And Jesus said to His disciples before ascending to heaven, "All authority has been given to Me in heaven and on earth. Go therefore and make disciples of all the nations" (Matthew 28:18-19).

Powerful praying and powerful witnessing are a result of having seen God in His sovereign reign. Power and authority do not belong to the United States or the Soviet Union. Power and authority belong to God. No government can stop the move of the Spirit of God. Laws can be passed, and the gospel can be forbidden, but the follower of Jesus can cross borders and liberate the captives through his prayers. There is nothing too difficult for God.

"HALLOWED BE THY NAME"

Jesus not only taught the disciples to focus on the goodness and greatness of God, but He also taught them to place their focus on the purity of God. He taught them to pray, "Our Father who art in heaven, *hallowed be Thy name*" (Matthew 6:9, emphasis added). The name of God is holy because He is holy. Names had a special meaning to the ancient Hebrew people. The name of a person many times represented the character of that person.

Jesus taught that when we come into the presence of God, we enter the presence of absolute purity. We can come into His presence only by the blood of the Lamb, with clean hands and a pure heart. We must enter His presence with a sense of reverence and awe, for God is holy.

We must open the door of prayer with our focus on God. We acknowledge His goodness, greatness, and purity with praise and thanksgiving. Something supernatural transpires when we offer to Him the sacrifice of praise from our hearts. God dwells in the midst of the praises of His people. And praise quickly becomes worship.

After Jesus taught His disciples to open the door of prayer with praise, He taught them to close the door of prayer in worship. The concluding principle of prayer is worship. Jesus taught His disciples to conclude in prayer with their hearts basking in the glory of God. He taught them to pray, "For thine is the kingdom, and the power, and the glory, forever. Amen" (Matthew 6:13).

When the believer has acknowledged God in the beauty of His holiness, the windows of heaven are opened. True worship bursts into the heart of man. Hallelujah is the primary word of worship in the Bible. Hallelujah leaps from the lips of the man or woman of prayer every time a new thought of the goodness, greatness, and majesty of God dawns upon his or her soul.

The need of this generation is for men and women who face life with their eyes fixed on the Savior. We need an army of worshipers. Our churches, communities, and countries will be transformed by men and women who have encountered the loving, eternal, holy Father. We need a generation of prayer warriors that will rearrange their priorities and see the face of God.

Charles Finney had his priorities straight and his focus upon God. He said, "I used to spend a great deal of time in prayer; sometimes, I thought, literally praying 'without ceasing.' I also found it very profitable, and felt much inclined to hold frequent days of private fasting. On those days I would seek to be entirely alone with God, and would generally wander off into the woods, or get into the meeting house, or somewhere away entirely by myself."[4]

---

4. Quoted in V. Raymond Edman, *Finney Lives On* (Minneapolis: Bethany, 1970), p. 44.

*Now that great man [David Brainerd] did his greatest
work by prayer. He was in the depths of those forests
alone, unable to speak the language of the Indians, but
he spent whole days literally in prayer. What was he
praying for? He knew he could not reach these savages,
for he did not understand their language. If he wanted
to speak at all, he must find somebody who could vaguely
interpret his thought. Therefore he knew that anything
he could do must be absolutely dependent upon God. So
he spent whole days in praying, simply that the power of
the Holy Ghost might come upon him so unmistakably
that these people would not be able to stand before him.*

*What was his answer? Once he preached through
a drunken interpreter, a man so intoxicated that he
could hardly stand up. This was the best he could do.
Yet scores were converted through that sermon. We can
account for it only that it was the tremendous power of
God behind him.*

(A. J. Gordon, quoted in E. M. Bounds,
The Weapon of Prayer [Baker, 1987])

*Thy kingdom come. Thy will be done, on earth as it is
in heaven.*

(Matthew 6:10)

7

Intercession: A Response to the Compassionate King

If one could travel throughout the world to visit the dwelling places of the kings and queens from all ages, he would discover an interesting accumulation of wealth, power, and history. Royalty lived quite differently from the common man. Some kings treated people with kindness. Other terrorized friends and foes alike.

There was a King, however, who visited earth two thousand years ago. He was no ordinary king. He was the King of all kings, the Lord of all lords. This King did not live in castles separated from common people. He once said that He had no place to lay His head. He was the compassionate King, the suffering King, the King who served His people. He was the King who loved the poor, the lame, the blind, and all of hurting humanity.

He came to establish His kingdom in the hearts of men and women. First He came to the Hebrew people, but they did not recognize Him because they were looking for a king who would drive the Romans out of their land. They wanted a king that would restore Israel by political and military power. But this King was not coming by might, or by power, but in the fullness and the anointing of the Spirit of God. The Jews anticipated the coming King, but when He came many of them denied Him, because they did not understand the nature of the King or His kingdom. They could not conceive that the long-awaited and promised King would be a friend to the bruised and brokenhearted.

Consequently, Jesus brought His kingdom to the common, simple people who would trust Him. He established His kingdom within the hearts of fishermen and tax collectors. He built His kingdom in the hearts of the needy and the lonely. He identified with hurting people.

Perhaps many in this generation would not recognize Jesus or His kingdom if He were to come today. Many hide behind stained-glass windows and sing about the royalty of Jesus. Yet they have isolated themselves from a hurting world. They recite their prayers, but it has been years since they have wept for the lost. Others only view Jesus as a mystical king. They can pray with great emotion and feeling, yet they find it difficult to reach out to neighbors, family, and friends who are about to enter eternity separated from God. Many who claim to follow Jesus have never prayed for the millions of Hindus in India who worship many different gods. Many have never prayed for the millions that have been taught in communist countries that there is no God.

"THY KINGDOM COME. THY WILL BE DONE, ON EARTH AS IT IS IN HEAVEN"

We need a fresh view of the compassionate King. We need to understand the nature of His kingdom. Jesus taught His disciples to pray, "Thy kingdom come. Thy will be done, on earth as it is in heaven."

What is the kingdom of God? There are three tenses in God's kingdom. The first is the past tense. It is a historical kingdom. John the Baptist preached, "Repent, for the kingdom of heaven is at hand" (Matthew 3:2). The kingdom was at hand because Jesus was about to be introduced to the world. And He would establish the kingdom of God in the hearts of men and women.

The second tense of the kingdom of God is the present tense. God has not changed. He is still building His kingdom on earth in the hearts of people. He loves the world. One of the most profound words in the Bible is the word *so*. John 3:16 says, "For God *so* loved the world" (emphasis added). The word *so* expresses the intensity of God's love for a rebellious humanity. We must understand how intensely God loves people. He wants to establish His rule in the hearts of people.

What did Jesus mean when He said, "Thy will be done, on earth as it is in heaven"? The Bible clearly states the will of God. It says that "the Lord is not slow about His promise, as some count slowness, but is patient toward you, not wishing for any to perish but for all to come to repentance" (2 Peter 3:9). When one prays for the will of God and the kingdom of God, he is in essence praying for the same thing. He is praying for Jesus to rule in the hearts of men and women.

The third tense of the kingdom of God is the future. The kingdom of God will culminate with the second return of the King. Jesus is coming again. We must prepare and pray for His coming. When we pray for His kingdom to come, we are essentially praying for two things. We are praying for the rule of God in the hearts of men and women and for the return of Christ.

The essence of "Thy kingdom come. Thy will be done, on earth as it is in heaven" is intercessory prayer. All prayer is a response to the nature and character of God. Intercession is a response to the compassionate sovereignty of Jesus. It is praying for men and women to come to know the rule of Jesus in their lives.

Intercessory prayer is hard work. It involves communion with the King and compassion for the multitudes. It is understanding the passion of Christ for souls. It is waiting on God to endue us with power from on high in order that we might lead those souls into the kingdom.

Those that have been most useful in reaping a harvest have always been men and women of intercessory prayer.

They cry to the Lord for the multitudes. They have no confidence in themselves to build the kingdom of God; they live in absolute dependence upon God.

David Brainerd was one such man. It has been said of Brainerd that he prayed in the forests until the snow melted under his feet. Yet Brainerd lived less than thirty years. From 1743 to 1747, he labored to reach the Indians in America for Christ. He constantly wrestled in prayer for the multitudes. His short life impacted the entire Christian world. A. J. Gordon said of him, "Now this man prayed in secret in the forest. A little while afterward, William Carey read his life, and by its impulse he went to India. Payson read it as a young man, over twenty years old, and he said that he had never been so impressed by anything in his life as by the story of Brainerd. Murray McCheyne said he likewise was impressed by it."[1]

Brainerd died in the home of Jonathan Edwards, who was mightily used of God in the first Great Awakening in America. Edwards said of Brainerd, "I praise God that it was in His Providence that he should die in my house, that I might hear his prayers, and that I might witness his consecration, and that I might be inspired by his example."[2]

George Whitefield was used mightily of God during the same period of time as Brainerd. Whitefield's methods were unusual because of his burden for the multitudes. He did not limit his preaching to the four walls of the church. He was the first of his generation to bring the message of Christ to the masses. Ten to twenty thousand regularly gathered to hear him. Some historians estimate occasional crowds of fifty thousand people would gather to hear him. He was a mighty instrument for God during the first Great Awakening. What was the secret of Whitefield? He prayed three times daily—in the morning, at noon, and at night. He shook America and England for Christ with his prayers.

1. Quoted in E. M. Bounds, *The Weapon of Prayer* (Grand Rapids: Baker, 1987), p. 135.
2. Ibid.

One hundred years later, God raised up another man to shake the English-speaking world for His glory. He was a shoe salesman from Chicago named Dwight L. Moody. Moody's burden for the kingdom of God began by reaching children off the streets of Chicago through Sunday school classes. Some of his first converts were, "Madden the Butcher, Red Eye, Rag-Breeches, Cadet, Black Stove Pipe, Old Man, Darby the Cobbler, Jackey Candles, Smikes, Butcher Lilray, Greenhorn, Indian, and Gilberic."[3]

Moody felt the heart of the compassionate King and began to reach those no one else cared about. His Sunday school class of street kids grew so large that President-elect Abraham Lincoln visited it. But Moody's heart grew larger than that Sunday school class. God broadened his heart to build the kingdom of God in Great Britain as well.

In a Glasgow auditorium, Moody preached to an overflow crowd of approximately 50,000. In London, he preached to more than 2,500,000. He preached in "Camberwell Hall, sixty meetings, 480,000 in attendance; Victoria Hall, forty-five meetings, 400,000; Royal Haymaker Opera House, sixty meetings, 330,000; Bow Road Hall, sixty meetings, 600,000; and Agricultural Hall, sixty meetings, 720,000."[4]

Moody's heart broke for those who did not know Jesus. What would happen in churches today if Sunday school teachers had the same burden as D. L. Moody? Who in this generation will weep for the unreached groups as Brainerd wept for the Indians? Who will pave new paths to reach the multitudes as Whitefield did two hundred years ago? The Bible says, "I searched for a man among them who should build up the wall and stand in the gap before Me for the land, that I should not destroy it; but I found no one" (Ezekiel 22:30). Will God find a man or woman to stand in the gap before Him in this generation?

3. Robert Flood and Jerry Jenkins, *Teaching the Word, Reaching the World* (Chicago: Moody, 1985), p. 21.
4. Ibid., p. 26.

A man in Romania who has made a great impact in the area of intercessory prayer interpreted for me when I preached in Bucharest. After the services we had a meal together in a restaurant with a few friends. As I looked out at the multitudes of people in Bucharest, a Scripture verse came to my mind that reveals Jesus' hurt for the city of Jerusalem. "O Jerusalem, Jerusalem, who kills the prophets and stones those who are sent to her! How often I wanted to gather your children together, the way a hen gathers her chicks under her wings, and you were unwilling" (Matthew 23:37). As I meditated on this passage, I realized that Jesus felt the same way about all of the cities of the world. I said, "O Bucharest, Bucharest."

Before I finished my statement, I looked over at my Romanian friend. Tears were running down his face. His heart broke for his people. The presence of God encircled each of us at the table. In those moments we felt the heart of the compassionate King. For several minutes we wept and were not able to speak.

We later went to a city located on the Danube River. Each evening at the conclusion of the evangelistic meetings we walked to the river. We spent a couple of hours there in prayer every night. I will never forget my friend lying prostrate on the ground, crying out to the Lord for his country, "Oh, God, if it takes the blood of the martyrs to bring our country under the rule of Christ, then I gladly offer my blood. But, please, let Your kingdom come and Your will be done in the hearts of the Romanian people." My life was deeply touched. I had prayed with a man who prayed with the heart of the compassionate King.

If we are to reach this generation for Christ, there must be men and women in every nation whose hearts hurt for their countrymen. Jesus had compassion for the multitudes two thousand years ago. And although the multitudes are greater today, He loves, cares for, and wants to save every individual. We need to look at the masses of humanity through the eyes of Jesus. We will see people—real people, hurting people. Too many of us see people only as objects. We need a fresh touch from God. We need to feel the heart of the compassionate King.

Perhaps some Christians will say, "I know that I should have a burden to pray for the world. But it is just not there. I am so busy with my own life and problems that I don't have time to pray for some people in a distant country that I will never meet." We must first recognize that we must be delivered from such self-centeredness. The goal of every Christian should be conformity unto the image of Jesus. And the heart of Jesus is for the world. We must confess our apathy as sin and repent of it.

There are four practical ways the compassionate King imparted His burden to me that I would recommend to the serious follower of Jesus. First, pray among the masses. Find a large group of people and walk among them silently praying, "God, let me see these people as You see them. Let me feel what You feel for them." Do this regularly and consistently. The Holy Spirit will begin to melt your heart.

This has been a practice of mine for many years. When I first began ministering on the streets of Chicago, I would occasionally drive to Chicago's O'Hare Airport. I would sit quietly in the airport and watch the crowds that passed me. I would silently ask God to break my heart for them. It was in these times that God began to give me a world vision.

I don't believe that we can fully appreciate God's heart for the masses unless we are among them. Prayer should not be a retreat from the world; it should be where we get our marching orders to go into the world. Many times the compassion of Christ grew out of His mingling with the masses. Matthew 9:36 says, "Seeing the multitudes, He felt compassion for them, because they were distressed and downcast like sheep without a shepherd." The heart of Jesus broke when He saw the multitudes.

Several years ago I walked through Alexanderplatz in East Berlin. There were one hundred thousand atheistic, communist youth gathered for a festival there. The youth represented countries from around the world. As I walked among those young people, God broke my heart. For one hour, I could only weep as the compassionate King touched my heart. Later that week, my colleagues and I were able to lead two hundred of those young people to Christ. We have seen thousands born into the kingdom of God in communist-dominated countries since that day. The reaping of the harvest began with the weeping of the soul.

God has continuously used this method of prayer to impart His vision to me. Students would benefit from walking through the halls of their schools in silent prayer, asking God to allow them to see their classmates as He sees them. Businessmen would benefit from spending a lunch hour walking through the business community in silent prayer. We need to walk throughout neighborhoods, both ghettos and suburbs, with a heart that is seeking the kingdom of God.

Second, find a Christian with a burning heart for souls. Meet with him and begin to pray for the lost. Compassion is more easily caught than taught. And the best training ground for prayer is prayer itself. Young Joshua led the children of Israel into the Promised Land. Moses met with God in a tent outside the camp. Exodus 33:11 says, "Thus the Lord used to speak to Moses face to face, just as a man speaks to his friend. When Moses returned to the camp, *his servant Joshua, the son of Nun, a young man, would not depart from the tent*" (emphasis added). Joshua learned the victory of prayer by spending time in prayer with a man of prayer.

Leo Humphrey of New Orleans, Louisiana, was the greatest soul winner I ever met. After my wife and I were married, we went to the French Quarter of New Orleans to work with Leo. He led drug addicts, motorcycle gang members, hippies, and some of the Mafia to Christ. Those were formative days in my Christian life. One could not help but catch the compassion of Christ while praying with Leo.

Third, become educated. Too many Christians only know about their own little world. We need to develop a global vision. There are many places that need the compassionate King. The serious intercessor should buy a world map and place it where it is accessible for prayer time. He should pray for one country each week and spend time researching information on that country. There is an excellent book entitled *Operation World*, by P. J. Johnstone (STL Publications). It gives excellent background, facts, and prayer burdens for countries around the world.

Finally, and most importantly, prayerfully study the gospels. Read through the gospel accounts with an eye to see the heart of Jesus for the multitudes. Behold the compassionate King, and your heart will begin to reach out to the host of hurting humanity. When we clearly see the King, our hearts will cry out, "Thy kingdom come. Thy will be done, on earth as it is in heaven."

All God's giants have been weak men, who did great things for God because they reckoned on His being with them. . . . Want of trust is at the root of almost all our sins and all our weaknesses, and how shall we escape it but by looking to Him and observing His faithfulness. The man who holds God's faithfulness will not be foolhardy or reckless, but he will be ready for every emergency.

(Hudson Taylor, quoted in Warren Wiersbe,
Walking with the Giants [Baker, 1976])

Give us this day our daily bread.

(Matthew 6:11)

8

Supplication: A Response to the Provision of God

When my wife, Tex, and I were married, we embarked on an adventure of faith. It has been an adventure that has continued to leave us with joy beyond description. We determined that we would trust God to meet our every need as we proclaimed the gospel. In the past twenty years, we have come to know God as Jehovah-Jireh, God our provider.

We felt the call of God into itinerant evangelism. Although we had no secure source of income, we were assured that this was the will of God. I read the life of George Mueller and was deeply moved by it. Mueller clothed thousands of children, accomplishing this without asking man to meet his financial needs. He looked to God alone as his source of supply. We likewise determined to ask no man for finances but to trust God in prayer.

Things went well for several months, but one morning we found ourselves in a financial crisis. The rent was due, but we had no money. I did not even have enough money to put gas in the car to drive to my next preaching engagement. We had no food in the cupboards, and the refrigerator was empty. Tex and I knelt by the bed and prayed. We prayed, "Oh, God, You called us to this ministry. We simply want to be obedient to You. It is only Your will that is important. If we are outside of Your will, then we will make whatever changes that are necessary to return to Your will. However, if we are in Your will, then we trust You to provide for our every need."

That day I went to the post office and found a check in the mail that was enough to pay our rent, buy groceries, and fill our car with gas. We rejoiced together and thanked God for His gracious supply.

We lived for several more months under the provision of God. But we again discovered one morning that our finances had been depleted. We hurriedly prayed again and told God we were trusting Him. As soon as we said, "Amen," I told Tex that I was going to the post office. I couldn't wait to see how much money would be there. When I got the mail I quickly searched for a check. Nothing. My heart sank.

Tex knew something was wrong when I returned home. I told her that no money came. We discussed the incident for some time that day and came to one of two conclusions: either we should not trust God in such a manner or something was wrong in our lives. We asked God to search our hearts and show us any defect. God showed me that I had not really trusted Him; I had trusted His method. God met our need during the first crisis through the mail, but my confidence on that day was placed in the mail rather than in God Himself.

I confessed this sin and repented of it. Later that day a campus minister told me that he received a check in the mail designated for me. I had preached several weeks prior in a church, and they wanted to send me a love offering. They did not know how to send it to me, so they sent it to my friend. It was just the amount we needed. God taught me a tremendous lesson through that experience. It is so easy to fix our eyes on God's method of provision rather than God. Our trust and confidence must always be in Him.

This book does not contain enough space to tell how God has provided for every need in order to accomplish His will. It has been humbling to see how God provided a truckload of baked goods for hungry people in the ghettos of Chicago. He allowed us to purchase an automobile for an evangelist in Eastern Europe, pay for a youth conference in India, support nationals in other nations, and preach in evangelistic campaigns on several continents. With hearts of gratitude, we have come to know God as our source of provision. God has met every need, and we have not had to ask man for anything. God is ready to reveal Himself to us as Jehovah-Jireh if we will only seek Him.

"GIVE US THIS DAY OUR DAILY BREAD"

Jesus taught His disciples to pray, "Give us this day our daily bread" (Matthew 6:11). This principle of prayer is the believer's response to the power and provision of God. The Father cares about the intimate details of the lives of His children. One hair cannot fall off the head of His child without His knowledge. He is able to meet every need of His children. The secret of kingdom living is childlike faith. This generation of Christians needs a fresh understanding of God, our provider.

It disturbs me to see a generation of evangelical Christians who have turned to mass-marketing techniques and manipulation for their financial needs. Preachers of the gospel speak of the life of faith. Yet many of them who speak with the greatest conviction about the power of God seem to beg the most. Great emotional pleas tell us that "thousands will go to hell if you do not write that letter and put that check in the mail." On the other hand, Christian seminars and gospel concerts have adopted a slogan that says, "Buy a ticket for ten dollars, and you can hear us sing or teach about Jesus." We are not far from saying, "You must pay if you are going to pray." Many speakers on the evangelical circuit charge large fees in order to preach the free grace of God.

All of this points us to the desperate spiritual state of evangelical Christianity. We have lost sight of God. God is searching for men and women of prayer who have learned to pray, "Give us this day our daily bread." The Father will not give a stone instead of bread to the man or woman of prayer. He is a good, loving, caring Father.

The church has been the weakest when she has lost sight of God, her provider. At that time the Father allows His light to shine in the heart of a man of prayer. Martin Luther was one such man. Luther was appalled by the fund-raising techniques of men such as Johann Dietzel. Dietzel was a master of emotional appeals, promising the release of relatives from purgatory if church members dropped their money into his chest. Luther decried such practices.

George Mueller refused to receive a salary from his first pastorate in England because the money came from pew rental. People had to pay for their seats in order to hear Mueller preach. Mueller gave three reasons for not participating in this common practice of fund-raising in his generation. He wrote, "Pew rents are, according to James 2:1-6, against the mind of the Lord, as, in general, the poor brother cannot have so good a seat as the rich. . . . I do not know whether he pays his money grudgingly, and of necessity, or cheerfully; but God loveth a cheerful giver. Nay, I know it to be a fact that sometimes it had not been convenient to individuals to pay the money when it had been asked for by the local brethren who collected it. . . . I felt that pew rents were a snare to the servant of Christ."[1]

Long after Mueller established these principles for his ministry, he could see the wisdom and provision of God. He stated, "We leaned on the arm of the Lord Jesus. It is now twenty-five years since we set out in this way, and we do not in the least regret the step we then took."[2]

Christians would do well to seriously ponder the objections of Luther and Mueller. If there is to be revival in this

1. George Mueller, *Autobiography of George Mueller*, ed. H. Lincoln Wayland (Grand Rapids: Baker, 1981), p. 66.
2. Ibid., p. 67.

generation, integrity must be restored. Often we preach that we have a great and wonderful God who is able and willing to meet the needs of His people, then we proceed with elaborate and sometimes emotional schemes to raise funds. As a result, the world has become cynical toward us—and rightly so.

Perhaps we ought to look to some of the poorer nations to see testimonies of churches that experience revival. Christians in Romania are suppressed. They have rationed food, power shortages, and little heat. Their church facilities are less than adequate. But the churches are growing, even though no one had a vision of Jesus telling Christians to dig deep into their pocketbooks and give. They do not have much materially, but they have the presence, power, and provision of God. The kingdom is being implanted in the hearts of a people who live in the darkness of atheism. Many of those people have come to know God as their provider. Perhaps we have attempted to manipulate God into funding our luxury and waste. Because God will have nothing to do with it, we must turn to our magnificent schemes to acquire wealth to spend on our every desire.

This evaluation of the church might seem harsh to some readers. However, it is not intended to be a finger pointed at the people of God. It is the simple cry of my heart with my finger pointed toward heaven. Look unto God. He is our provider. Call unto Him, and He will meet every need of our lives. The God of Mueller is the God of this generation.

Some may object to such praying based on two lines of reasoning. First, some will say, "We do not live in the times of George Mueller. Our society has changed. Life is more complicated. We do not live in an oppressed society. Things are different in Western Europe and North America than in communist-dominated Romania. We live in a system of free enterprise. These methods of fund-raising are part of a culture that allows such freedom." I must raise a loud protest. Our God has not changed! Times and cultures change, but

God does not. If we have become so full of schemes that we do not need to lean on the strong arms of Jesus, then we have become the most desperate of all people.

The second objection is more difficult. Some will say, "I have attempted to raise funds for the work of God through prayer alone. But it did not work. Because the work of God is more important than the manner in which I pray, I have found it expedient and more practical to make appeals to man for money. Paul appealed to people for money in the Bible. Why should I not do the same?"

I would agree that it is not antibiblical to appeal for finances. I do object, however, to the gross imbalance that has crept into the church. Confidence has been transferred from God to the methods of man. There have been such outlandish public appeals made for funds over television, radio, and in the pulpits of our churches that it has become an embarrassment to evangelical Christianity.

Why is it that prayer has not worked for some people? Why do some good ministries always lack funds? Many pray, but there is seemingly no provision. This is a question that has plagued me for years. Although I do not have a lot of solutions to this dilemma, I do believe that there are some biblical insights that will help us understand the problem.

First, one cannot pray, "Give us this day our daily bread," until he has prayed, "Thy will be done, on earth as it is in heaven." The provision of God is built upon the reign of God. God has no obligation to finance that which is outside of His will. There must be a deep commitment to the will of God before there can be confidence in the provision of God. The safest place in the world to live is in the will of God. There are many good and godly things that we can do in life, but the will of God is always the best. God may withhold His provision from that which is good in order that we can have His best.

Faith in the New Testament is often expressed as obedience in the Old Testament. For instance, the Old Testament speaks of Abraham's obedience to the call of God to go to a foreign land. The New Testament describes the same incident in terms of the faith of Abraham. In other words, faith and obedience are precipitated by the directive of God. It would have been foolish for Abraham to strike out on such a journey without a clear directive from God. He could believe and trust God to meet his every need because he was clearly in the will of God.

If we are to live with the provision of God, then we must dwell in the will of God. A businessman is to walk by faith as much as someone with a ministry such as George Mueller. Mueller could trust God for His supply because he had a directive from God to build orphans' homes. The doctor who administers medicine because of God's leadership in his life can look to God as his source of supply. The mechanic that repairs automobiles because God has called him to be a light to the world in an auto garage can rest assured of God's provision. He must understand that his paycheck is ultimately not from the owner of the garage but from the Creator of the universe. It is God that gives him the health, abilities, skills, and knowledge to perform that work. He must look to God for his provision daily as much as George Mueller did for those orphan children. The only question to be resolved is, "Is what I am doing the will of God?" An affirmative answer to that question places us in the position to trust God for His provision.

If one is to trust God for His provision, then he must not only have a commitment to the will of God but also an understanding and commitment to the kingdom of God. He must pray, "Thy kingdom come." He is then in a position to pray, "Give us this day our daily bread." Many seem not to have God's provision because they do not have God's priority. Jesus said, "But seek first His kingdom and His righteousness; and all these things shall be added to you" (Matthew 6:33).

There must be some serious, critical questions resolved concerning the kingdom of God and the evangelical church in this generation if we are to experience a spiritual awakening. For instance, what does a Christian amusement park have to do with the kingdom of God? Perhaps the greatest scandal of this century is that American Christians poured hundreds of millions of dollars into such a park while millions of people starve in Africa. It is unthinkable to believe that while radical Islam and militant Communism threaten the kingdom of God in much of the world, Christians should have a first-class recreation area.

This is not a statement against family recreation. The family does not need to isolate itself from the world. The world needs to see a happy, healthy Christian family that can enjoy one another. However, we must understand that the evangelical church is on a destructive course of misplaced priorities. And we must understand that God has made no promise to provide for such follies. As long as the kingdom of God has lost its priority in the church of this century, we will continue to hear begging and pleading for resources.

We must learn to recognize the difference between a need and a want. God has promised to meet every need of the Christian. He has never promised to bathe us in luxury. Too many Christians believe that God is obligated to finance every desire of their lives. We have forgotten the words of the apostle Paul, "I have learned to be content in whatever circumstances I am. I know how to get along with humble means, and I also know how to live in prosperity; in any and every circumstance I have learned the secret of being filled and going hungry, both of having abundance and suffering need" (Philippians 4:11-12).

There is much talk about the quality of life in various nations. The Communists say that the West has a poor quality of life because of high crime, drug abuse, and the breakdown of the family. The West says that the quality of life in a communist country is poor because of the lack of consumer goods, religious and intellectual repressions, and alcohol abuse. But my experience has found miserable people in both communist and capitalist countries. Quality of life is not derived from circumstances, cultures, or political ideologies. Quality of life is found in the kingdom of God. Romans 14:17 states, "For the kingdom of God is not eating and drinking, but righteousness and peace and joy in the Holy Spirit." Quality of life can be found in the inner man. God will not only provide us with daily bread for our basic human needs, but He will become the Bread of Life to our souls. The greatest need of our lives is God Himself. He will feed us with manna from His kingdom—righteousness, peace, and joy.

Sometimes God will reduce His outward provision for a ministry in order to expand the inner character of man. That is why the apostle Paul could be content in a jail cell or preaching to the masses. He knew that the greatest need of his life was for God to feed his soul with the bread of heaven. The bread of heaven would enable him to grow into the likeness of Christ.

There is one final reason that many in this generation have not experienced the provision of God: indebtedness. The world lives and runs on the principle of debt. The Christian, however, must live in a position of availability to God and man. When one is in debt, he is not totally free. He is in bondage to another man. A follower of Jesus ought to live in such a manner that if Jesus says, "Go," then he is free to go. Many Christians could not give themselves to kingdom service even if they knew it to be the will of God. They are bound by indebtedness.

Tex and I decided not to go in debt when we were first married. We have tried to live by that principle. It has liberated us from financial pressures on our marriage and given us the freedom to do whatever God speaks to our hearts. I have seen others attempt the same type of ministry. However, they have grown weary under financial stress and quit. Many times, the stress was there because they brought a heavy load of indebtedness with them into the ministry. They violated the principle of, "Owe nothing to anyone except to love one another" (Romans 13:8).

Hudson Taylor was converted to Christ at seventeen. God worked in Taylor's life to build Christlike character. He became a man of intercessory prayer. He went to China and trusted God alone to meet his every need on the mission field. His philosophy was, "God's work done in God's way will never lack God's supply." Taylor said concerning indebtedness, "And what does going into debt really mean? It means that God has not supplied your need. . . . If we can only wait right up to the time, God cannot lie, God cannot forget: He is pledged to supply all our need."[3]

Perhaps not everyone will agree with my premise. One who has an objective view of finances, however, must confess that world government is in great danger because of indebtedness. Families are in trouble because of indebtedness. It is my conviction that many ministries are in trouble because of indebtedness. Evangelical Christians must take a closer look at the principle of financial freedom. God is our provider. If the provision is not there when we need it, I am convinced that the fault does not lie with God. Man must carefully examine his own life-style and measure it against the Word of God. We can expect the provision of God when our lives line up with the Word of God.

Our God is faithful. When we have a commitment to His will, His kingdom, and His Word, He will meet our every need. The most secure place in the world is the secret chamber of prayer. It is in that place that the man or woman of prayer meets Jehovah-Jireh.

3. Quoted in Warren Wiersbe, *Walking with the Giants* (Grand Rapids: Baker, 1976), p. 66.

*Beloved followers of Jesus, called to manifest His like-
ness to the world, learn that as forgiveness of your sins
was one of the first things Jesus did for you, forgiveness
of others is one of the first things that you can do for
Him. And remember that to the new heart, there is a joy
even sweeter than that of being forgiven, even the joy of
forgiving others.*

    (Andrew Murray, *The Best of Andrew Murray*
                  [Baker, 1978])

*Forgive us our debts, as we also have forgiven our
debtors.*

                  (Matthew 6:12)

9

Confession: A Response to the Holiness and Grace of God

All prayer is a response to the attributes and character of God. The more clearly we see Him, the more powerfully we can pray. We become like Him because we know Him intimately. There is one attribute of God that adjectives cannot adequately describe: the grace of God. It has been the theme of all the great preachers since the book of Acts. Men such as the apostle Paul, Augustine, Martin Luther, John Calvin, George Whitefield, and Charles Spurgeon have been motivated by this characteristic. Their ministries, lives, and prayers were revolutionized by a clear understanding of this attribute.

Hymn writer John Newton could find no better way to express his feelings about this quality of the Creator of the universe than to write, "Amazing grace, how sweet the sound!" Our God is the God of grace and mercy. The one characteristic that separates heathen religion and pagan praying from New Testament Christianity is grace. The first attribute of God that one comes to know at the experience of salvation is that of grace. We are saved by grace, kept by grace, and will continue to grow by grace.

The true man or woman of prayer is one that intimately knows this part of God's character. Prayer is coming into the presence of God. It is only by the grace of God that we can stand before a holy God. The throne in heaven is described as a throne of grace.

Our confidence in prayer is established in our hearts because He is full of grace. Grace is His favor bestowed upon us simply because He loves us. He receives us at His throne not because of our performance but because of His grace bestowed upon us through Jesus. Hebrews 4:15-16 states, "For we do not have a high priest who cannot sympathize with our weaknesses, but one who has been tempted in all things as we are, yet without sin. Let us therefore draw near with confidence to the throne of grace, that we may receive mercy and may find grace to help in time of need."

When Jesus came into my life and set me free from the bondage of guilt and sin, I began to discover the adventure of prayer. Two friends and I would meet early each morning near the state capitol building in Baton Rouge, Louisiana. We memorized Scripture verses together and spent time alone in prayer. As a new Christian, I was continually overwhelmed that I could enter the presence of holy, almighty God. There was continually the joy of prayer that flowed from the throne of grace.

Many have struggled with the balance of the holiness of God and the grace of God. Christians seem to divide into one of two camps: holiness or grace. There is continual tension between the two views. A man once said to me, "If I must fall on the side of one of the two tensions, then I would rather fall on the side of grace." But we must never fall to the side of either one; we need a balanced view of God. Holiness and grace are two different sides of the same coin. The coin is not a legitimate coin without both sides. An unbalanced view of God is an illegitimate understanding of the nature of God.

"FORGIVE US OUR DEBTS, AS WE ALSO HAVE FORGIVEN OUR DEBTORS"

Jesus taught His disciples to pray, "Forgive us our debts, as we also have forgiven our debtors" (Matthew 6:12). The principle of forgiveness is a response to the holiness and grace of God. From the beginning of these principles, Jesus placed the focus of the hearts of the disciples upon the holiness of God as He taught them to pray, "Hallowed be Thy name." It is the holiness of God that compels our hearts to cry out for the grace of God.

Holiness produces humility of heart. Grace is then applied to the heart of humility. The depth of our confession is only as great as the clarity of our view of the holiness of God. Too much confession is rooted in comparison to other people. We can always justify our attitudes and actions by thinking we are not as bad as some other Christians. Such comparison only produces pride in our hearts. However, when we focus on the holy God, we must cry out with Isaiah, "Woe is me, for I am ruined! Because I am a man of unclean lips, and I live among a people of unclean lips; for my eyes have seen the King, the Lord of hosts" (Isaiah 6:5).

Isaiah had a vision of the glory of God. That vision produced a deep brokenness, confession, and repentance in his life. There were several characteristics of Isaiah's prayer that are important for us to recognize. They are the ingredients that result from a clear view of the holiness and grace of God.

Isaiah was transparent in his prayer. He did not try to impress God or anyone else with his piety. He was honest. He knew that God was able to search the heart of man. Because he knew that only truth would be pleasing to God, he was willing to admit his wrong.

This is one of the most difficult aspects of prayer. We live in a world that teaches us how to wear masks in order to impress others. We attempt to carry our masks into prayer.

God's glory is only manifest, however, to the heart that has taken off its mask. We must come to the chamber of prayer with humility, honesty, and transparency.

Matthew Henry commented on the confession of Isaiah, saying, "And one would think, he should have said, 'Happy am I, for ever happy; nothing now shall trouble me, nothing shall make me blush or tremble'; on the contrary he cries out, 'Woe is me, for I am undone.' "[1] There is no place for the mask of spiritual arrogance when one enters the presence of the God of glory.

Isaiah was also specific in his confession. There was a particular area of his life that needed the cleansing of God—the sin of an impure tongue. When he saw a holy, righteous, and glorious God, he could not help but ask God to purge and cleanse his lips. The high praises of God could never come from impure lips. Isaiah had an immensely high view of God. Such a view will spotlight the impurities of our lives.

Many Christians pray, "Forgive me of my sins." But such praying produces little repentance. Repentance is the forerunner of forgiveness, and God desires to forgive and cleanse His children. He loves us and wants to remove the burden of guilt. But we must be specific in our confession and repentance of sin.

The great hindrance to man's fellowship with God is guilt. Guilt is mean and knows no end to its torture and destruction. Many suffer in hospitals from the agony of guilt. Many psychological and emotional disorders grow in a heart that has been planted with the seeds of guilt. Guilt can destroy a marriage, prompt suicide, or distort the human personality.

Guilt must be removed from our lives if we are to experience victory. There are two types of guilt: false guilt and true guilt. Quite often the man or woman of prayer struggles with false guilt. False guilt is general in nature and has

1. Matthew Henry, *Matthew Henry's Commentary on the Whole Bible*, vol. 2 (Grand Rapids: Guardian Press, 1976), p. 676.

Satan as its source. Satan, the accuser of the brethren, accuses us in general terms. He whispers in our ears, "You are no good. How can you pray? You are not worthy."

The one who listens to such accusations will never become mighty in prayer. How can one repent of being "no good"? Only Jesus is worthy. Our access to God is never based on the worthiness of man; our access is based on the blood of Jesus. It is only by grace that we can approach God. Therefore, we must reject all false guilt when we pray.

The second type of guilt is true guilt. Many feel guilty when they pray because they *are* guilty. The difference between an accusation of Satan and conviction from the Holy Spirit is this: Satan's accusation is general, thus repentance is impossible. The Holy Spirit's conviction is specific and leads to repentance. Confession of sin is not to be morbid self-introspection. Confession of sin is the result of the light of God shining in our hearts. He knows our ways. He leads us down the path of repentance into forgiveness. The great English preacher Charles Haddon Spurgeon said, "Repentance and forgiveness are riveted together by the eternal purpose of God. . . . In the very nature of things, if we believe in the holiness of God it must be that if we continue in our sin and will not repent of it, we cannot be forgiven but must reap the consequences of our obstinacy."[2]

When there is sincere confession and true repentance, there will be a release of the rivers of grace upon the soul. As the soul of a man is flooded with divine grace, a new confidence begins to swell in his heart. There is a new boldness to approach God. He is clean and pure. And the pure in heart are blessed because they shall see God.

Prayer reaches a high level of intimacy. Love and gratitude flow from the heart that has been graced by God. The burden is lifted, and a quiet "hallelujah" is lifted from the

2. C. H. Spurgeon, *All of Grace* (Springdale, Pa.: Whitaker House, 1981), pp. 94-95.

lips of the man who walks and lives in the forgiveness of God.

When one has been forgiven, he has a living well of grace within him. The overflow of his life is grace. He has been graced by God and now has a supernatural ability to grace others. Prayer takes the disciples of Jesus before the throne of grace. Therefore, the outstanding character quality of the man or woman of prayer should be grace.

John describes Jesus in his gospel account by writing, "The Word became flesh, and dwelt among us, and we beheld His glory, glory as of the only begotten from the Father, full of grace and truth" (John 1:14). The grace of God flows from the glory of God. When one beholds Jesus, he sees the glory of God. And grace flows majestically from his life. When one is conformed into His image, he will be described as a person of grace.

This is why Jesus not only taught the disciples to pray, "Forgive us our debts," but He added, "as we also have forgiven our debtors" (Matthew 6:12). Forgiveness toward others is the overflow of the life that has been forgiven. When one refuses to forgive others, there is a hindrance to the flow of grace in his life. He ceases to live by the principle of grace and begins to live by the principle of performance. Thus, the prayer life is thwarted. It is impossible to come before the throne of grace and, at the same time, refuse to allow the grace of God to flow through us to others. We cannot receive grace from God and refuse grace to others. That would be living by two conflicting principles.

There are two poisonous and deadly attitudes that the Christian can harbor: guilt and bitterness. Guilt is the result of our failure; however, bitterness is much more subtle. Bitterness is the result of the actions and words of someone who has failed us. Guilt is the result of our wrong, but bitterness is the result of someone else's wrong.

The man of prayer must deal with both deadly sins. Both are opposed to the throne of heaven. And grace cannot flow into the heart that acts on the principle of performance.

In Matthew 18:22-35 Jesus explains the principle of grace and forgiveness. In His parable there were two slaves. Although the first slave owed his master approximately $10 million, the master forgave the first slave his debt.

The first slave then found his fellow slave, who owed him approximately one day's wages. The first slave refused to live by grace and would not forgive his fellow slave of his debt. When the master heard that the original slave was no longer living by grace, he turned the slave over to the tormentors.

The master in Jesus' parable represents God. God is a God of grace, and He is willing to forgive. The follower of Jesus is like the first slave. He has been graced by God—forgiven a debt that would be impossible to repay. When the follower of Jesus refuses to forgive his brother in Christ, however, he ceases to live by grace. His heart is tormented. The tormentor many times is called "bitterness."

Bitterness is evil and destructive. It has caused many murders and wars. It has broken marriages and divided churches. Bitterness has separated the believer from the power of God. True power is not in the Kremlin or the White House; true power is in the throne room of heaven. And God's throne is a throne of grace. Bitterness cannot walk into the presence of grace. Consequently, bitterness renders the prayer life of the disciple ineffective.

I have heard Christians say, "I cannot forgive. You don't understand the depth of hurt that was inflicted upon me." I must disagree. A true believer *can* forgive. It is the ability to forgive that distinguishes the Christian from the world.

We must understand the depth of the hurt that we have inflicted upon the heart of God. It was neither Jews nor Roman soldiers that kept Jesus on that cross; He could have called ten legions of angels to rescue Him. It was our sins.

Think of the horribleness of that statement. The pure, perfect, altogether lovely Son of God was kept on that cruel cross by our rebellion. Yet the Father looks at us and says, "Forgiven." The grace of God is marvelous!

No one has ever sinned against anyone with the same depth that we have sinned against God. There is much human tragedy that takes place in our lives, but nothing is as tragic as what we have done to the Son of God. Yet the Father has placed in our hearts a well of grace, and an eternal river of forgiveness flows into that well from the throne of heaven. When someone sins against us, we only need to dip a bucket of faith into the well of grace. We can raise from our hearts forgiveness that flows from the throne of heaven. In the name of Jesus, we can give our worst enemies a refreshing cup of forgiveness.

At that moment something supernatural transpires. That river of forgiveness begins to flood our souls. The deep scar of hurt begins to be healed by the salve of grace. And there is no limit to the grace and forgiveness that is found at the throne of heaven. The more forgiveness that we give out, the more forgiveness that flows into our hearts. There is an eternal supply found at the throne of grace. For that reason prayer becomes a great adventure. It transports us to the throne of grace.

On his knees the believer is invincible.
> (C. H. Spurgeon, *Final Manifesto*
> [Grace Publications, 1972])

Do not lead us into temptation, but deliver us from evil.
> (Matthew 6:13)

10

Warfare: A Response to the Protection and Power of God

Several years ago I sat in the home of a dynamic young Christian leader in a country where Christians are severely persecuted. His telephone was hidden under one of the cushions of his couch because he believed it was bugged. Although he had been interrogated by the secret police several times, he remained faithful to the Lord.

This man said to me, "When I lose the sense of being in a battle, I become apathetic. I must live with a keen realization that I am in a battle for the souls of men." As I listened to him, I realized that most Christians in the West do not even realize that there is a battle. The church must be aroused from her slumber. We must be awakened and put on our battle gear. We must move out like a mighty army for the glory of God. There are nations to be conquered, hearts to be won, and souls to be claimed. We must put on our fighting gear in the secret chamber of prayer. It is there that we receive our marching orders.

Perhaps the state of the church can be best described by two men. One is called Disciple, and the other is called Enemy. Disciple is a foot soldier in the army of the Lord. He has everything he needs to defend himself and defeat Enemy. He has defensive equipment that cannot be penetrated.

His equipment includes the belt of truth. The belt of truth has three places where the remainder of the gear can be fastened to it. First, he can fasten it to the truth about Jesus, who is the exact representation of the nature of God. Second, he can fasten it to the truth about life. Psalm 119:160 says, "Thy word is truth." Third, he can fasten it to the truth about himself. "If we say that we have no sin, we are deceiving ourselves, and the truth is not in us" (1 John 1:8). He is well-equipped with the belt of truth.

Disciple also has the breastplate of righteousness. He knows that his righteousness is nothing more than a bunch of dirty rags. Therefore, he has clothed himself with the strong and mighty righteousness of the Lord that is found in Jesus Christ. The vital areas of his life are protected by the righteousness of Jesus.

He has placed on his feet sandals called "peace." The sandals of peace are the result of his faith in Jesus Christ (Romans 5:1). They enable Disciple to be decisive and move quickly when Enemy attacks.

In addition to this, he has the shield of faith. His shield was invented, designed, created, and completed by the Lord Jesus, who is "the author and perfecter of faith" (Hebrews 12:2).

Finally, he has the helmet of salvation. The helmet offers total protection. It protects him in the past from the penalty of sin. It protects him in the present from the power of sin. And it will protect him in the future from the presence of sin.

The summation of all this armor is Jesus. Prayer is a time where Disciple clothes himself with Jesus. He must allow Jesus to fill and engulf every area of his life. He does not have to be defeated by Enemy; Jesus has given him everything that he needs for a life of victory.

Early in my Christian life I had the privilege of listening to Oswald J. Smith. He told a story of a girl who was converted under his ministry. He asked the young girl what she was going to do when the devil came to knock at the door of her heart. The girl thought for a moment and with a smile replied, "I guess I'll just have to send Jesus to the door."

That girl knew the secret of the Christian battle. Disciple needs to simply put on Jesus and stand firm in Him. The victory is the Lord's! Enemy and all of the demons of hell have to flee in the face of Jesus. He is the conquering Captain.

There is one important factor that we must realize. All of this armor Disciple has clothed himself with so far is defensive in nature. Although Jesus wants Disciple to be protected from Enemy, He also desires Disciple to be on the offensive. He wants Disciple to tear down the strongholds of Enemy and capture the hearts of those that have been enslaved by him.

Jesus has given Disciple one piece of equipment that is powerful for tearing down the strongholds of Enemy: the sword of the Spirit, the Word of God. This sword can pierce the most hardened heart and bring liberty and freedom from the bondage of sin.

There is one important fact, however, that Disciple must never forget. The Word of God is the sword of the *Spirit.* It is not the sword of human flesh and effort. It can only be properly used in battle by the Holy Spirit. Many have been turned further away from the gospel by someone who tried to browbeat them into the kingdom with his Bible. Others have been gently led to receive eternal life by properly using the sword, the Word of God.

Only the Holy Spirit can properly utilize Scripture. He knows the deep needs of every captive. The only question to be resolved is this: How does Disciple place his life under the control of the Holy Spirit so that God can use him effectively in the offensive battle? Disciple is told what to do in Ephesians 6:18 once he is clothed with all of his armor and has the sword in his hand: "With all prayer and petition pray at all times in the Spirit, and with this in view, be on the alert with all perseverance and petition for all the saints." Prayer places Disciple at God's disposal. The greatest power that Disciple has in this battle is made available to him through prayer.

Enemy is aware of this source of power, but he knows that his power is no match for the power of God. Therefore, he has devised a scheme. He sends one of his agents to attempt to render useless the power source of Disciple. The agent's name is Habit. Habit attempts to fill Disciple's time with things that are of no eternal value. Habit attempts to fill Disciple's time with television. Habit helps Disciple to climb the ladder of success. He even helps fill Disciple's life with religious activities.

Enemy and Habit, however, begin to tremble when Disciple rearranges his schedule. They must flee when Disciple seeks the face of God. They know that their kingdom of darkness in the hearts of men will soon have the light of God shining into it. Prayer places Disciple in a position to turn the kingdom of darkness into a kingdom of light, for prayer can move the glory of God into the hearts of men and women.

"Do Not Lead Us into Temptation"

Jesus taught His disciples to pray "Do not lead us into temptation, but deliver us from evil" (Matthew 6:13) so that they could begin their life of prayer with their focus upon God. But in this final principle, He teaches them that prayer will also touch the deepest needs of the human heart. He is teaching the disciples that prayer is a response to the protection and the power of God.

This final principle of prayer is a realization of the triumphant nature of God. The disciple sees the victory that is in Jesus Christ over all of the forces of hell. In the secret chamber of prayer, the follower of Christ begins to experience the twofold victory of the Lord. The first part of that victory stems from a clear view of God, who leads and shepherds His people. The second aspect of the triumph of the prayer warrior is his vision of the power of God to deliver His people from the forces of evil.

"Do not lead us into temptation" is a basic commitment of the Christian in prayer to the leadership of the Holy Spirit. The Christian sees the Lord as his Shepherd. He knows that Christ is a Good Shepherd. The Good Shepherd will not lead the sheep off a cliff! He will not lead the sheep into the pits of destruction. Therefore, the believer must commit himself to the leadership of the Good Shepherd. This is a time for the believer to commit his time, activities, and relationships to the leadership of the Holy Spirit.

Moses understood the importance of such praying. He met with God in a tent outside the camp, where the multitudes dwelt. But before he returned to his daily responsibilities and tasks, he cried unto the Lord, "If Thy presence does not go with us, do not lead us up from here" (Exodus 33:15). Moses knew there would be difficulties, problems, and trials along the way. He knew that he needed the leadership of God.

Jesus was not teaching the disciples that there would be no struggles for the man of prayer; He was teaching the opposite. He taught the disciples that they needed the leadership of God in the midst of the trials. Otherwise, they would fall into the snare of the devil. Satan is cunning, and he continuously sets traps for the Christian. He does everything within his power to tempt and defeat the Christian. The man of prayer, however, can rest assured of God's protection.

I discussed this aspect of prayer with Romanian believers who had emigrated to the United States. One of them made an interesting statement about the cunning ways of Satan. He said, "In Romania, Satan is like a roaring lion. He attempts to intimidate Christians with persecution and fear. But in America, Satan is like an angel of light. His method is compromise and complacency. I find it more difficult to deal with an angel of light than to deal with a roaring lion.

At least you know who the enemy is when it's a roaring lion. However, one must really have the leadership of the Holy Spirit when he deals with an angel of light."

If the follower of Jesus is to live under the leadership of the Holy Spirit, he must remove every hindrance to God's leading. For example, he cannot pray, "Lead me not into the temptation of lust," and watch sexually provocative movies. He cannot pray, "Lead me away from impure thought," and read literature that is profane and impure. One cannot submit to the leadership of God and retain habits that grieve the Holy Spirit. God is ready to lead when the Christian is ready to follow.

Prayer is not a plea for the absence of trials, but it is supplication for God's leadership in the midst of trials. Alan Redpath gives a concise paraphrase of the meaning of the phrase "lead us not into temptation." He writes, "It is the one negative petition in the family prayer; it is the one thing we dread more than anything else. I could paraphrase it this way as I often do as I seek the Lord myself: 'Lord, I am weak, and I would avoid every temptation of the devil if I could. I do not ask to be exempt from trial, because that would not be good for me, but Lord, if today there is to be put in my path an inducement to sin, Lord Jesus, then lead me through. Take my hand, and keep me near to You, Lord Jesus. I don't ask to be free from the furnace of testing, but, O God, I desperately need Your presence through the fire.' "[1]

Temptation will always confront us, and we must understand two truths about it if we are to experience victory. First, temptation is not sin, but it is an inducement to sin. How we respond is important. We can yield to the inducement, or we can yield to the leadership of the Holy Spirit. Second, it is important to understand the source of temptation and the means by which it attempts to induce us. God does not tempt His children to sin. Satan is the tempter, the

1. Alan Redpath, *Victorious Praying* (Old Tappan, N.J.: Revell, 1957), p. 101.

source of evil. Satan uses the world and the flesh to tempt the follower of Jesus. We must never forget, however, that Satan is a defeated foe.

The system of the world is contrary to the principles and character of God. Because the believer lives within that system, Satan continuously tries to seduce him with the lusts of the world system. The fleshly part of man has been affected by the Fall. The "old man" lives by this principle. It is the principle of living by one's outward desires and drives rather than by inward obedience to God. The Christian must yield himself to God in prayer, choosing not to be conformed to this world but to crucify the flesh and its lusts. One must make these daily choices in the secret chamber of prayer. When one wholly yields himself to God, he will then be able to walk and live under the leadership of the Holy Spirit.

"But Deliver Us from Evil"

We now come to the second principle of spiritual warfare, "But deliver us from evil [or the evil one]." There are two extreme views concerning this principle.

The first view looks for a demon under every tree. Many in this generation use this principle to cast demons out of Christians. We hear of Christians who have been delivered from everything ranging from the demon of lust to the demon of gluttony. Many of these well-meaning Christians, however, need another deliverance from the same demon a few weeks or months later. They seem to be haunted by these same desires and are never able to find total victory.

There is a good reason for the lack of victory: the flesh is impossible to cast out. It must be daily crucified. Satan can tempt the believer at the point of the flesh, but Satan and the flesh are not the same. If one closely studies the deeds of the flesh, it becomes obvious that much of what is called "deliverance ministry" has missed the basic problem and solution for victory in the life of the believer.

Galatians 5:19-21 clearly states the deeds of the flesh: "Immorality, impurity, sensuality, idolatry, sorcery, enmities, strife, jealously, outbursts of anger, disputes, dissensions, factions, envying, drunkenness, carousing, and things like these." Many of these deeds are being cast out of Christians as demons. The Christian will never know victory over these deeds, however, until he owns up to his own responsibility for such deeds. Immorality and impurity are choices that people make. Satan is ultimately the seducer; however, the Christian is the one who makes the choice. He either chooses to yield to the Holy Spirit and crucify the lusts of the flesh, or he chooses to yield to the deeds of the flesh. He will have to make that choice as long as he dwells in his mortal body on this sin-cursed earth.

That is why prayer is vitally important. Prayer enables the Christian to put on the whole armor of God and make no room for the deeds of the flesh. Prayer enables the believer to prepare for the battle that will take place as he goes into a world that is contrary to the nature of God. Prayer brings the follower of Christ under the leadership of the Holy Spirit. And prayer gives him confidence in the truth of the apostle Paul's statement, "Walk by the Spirit, and you will not carry out the desire of the flesh" (Galatians 5:16).

A second view is contrary to the principle, "But deliver us from evil." This view is a type of Christian humanism that recognizes only the will of man and ignores the spiritual battle taking place. The Christian life is presented only as making the right choices in life. The spiritual dimension of the Christian life is ignored.

A battle rages for the souls of men. The man of prayer will recognize that the forces of hell will do everything to keep men in bondage to their sins. The man of prayer understands that "our struggle is not against flesh and blood, but against the rulers, against the powers, against the world forces of this darkness, against the spiritual forces of wickedness in the heavenly places" (Ephesians 6:12). The man or woman of prayer must learn to wrestle in prayer against the spiritual forces of wickedness.

God is assembling an army of prayer warriors in this generation. The Spirit is whispering in the hearts of men and women, "Pray! Pray!" He is calling believers to put on the whole armor of God. He is our shepherd and protector, our deliverer and strength. We do not have to fear the enemy. We can storm the gates of hell on our knees and rescue multitudes that are perishing.

Charles Haddon Spurgeon said, "We are rowing like lifeboat men upon a stormy sea, and we are hurrying to yonder wreck, where men are perishing. If we may not draw that old wreck to shore, we will at least, by the power of God, rescue the perishing, save life, and bear the redeemed to the shores of salvation. Our mission, like our Lord's, is to gather out the chosen of God from among men, that they may live to the glory of God."[2]

"FOR THINE IS THE KINGDOM, AND THE POWER, AND THE GLORY, FOREVER. AMEN."

Nothing brings more joy than to know that God is our deliverer—a mighty deliverer to all who call upon His name. We must look unto Him to deliver us from the snare of the enemy as we walk in this sin-cursed world. And we, through prayer, can trust Him to deliver the multitudes from their bondage of sin. Worship will flood our souls as we behold God as our protector and power. We will humbly adore Him, crying, "For Thine is the kingdom, and the power, and the glory, forever. Amen."

---

2. C. H. Spurgeon, *Final Manifesto* (San Marcos, Calif.: Grace Publications, 1972), p. 59.

Part 3
Prayer and Spiritual Awakening

Oh, that Thou wouldst rend the heavens and come down.
(Isaiah 64:1)

The history of revivals brings that out very clearly for God often acts in a most unusual manner, and produces revival and promotes it and keeps it going, not necessarily through ministers but perhaps through people who may have regarded themselves as very humble and unimportant members of the Christian church.

(Martyn Lloyd-Jones, *Revival* [Crossway, 1987])

He brought us out from there in order to bring us in, to give us the land which He had sworn to our fathers. So the Lord commanded us to observe all these statutes, to fear the Lord God for our good always and for our survival, as it is today.

(Deuteronomy 6:23-24)

11

Historical Awakening and Prayer

The Christian church has a tremendous history of revivals and evangelism. There have been times, however, when it seemed as though a cloud of darkness hovered over the church. The church appeared to lose her effectiveness and even her message. She seemed to lose her saltiness, and her light burned dimly.

During those times of spiritual apathy and darkness the Holy Spirit would quietly stir in the heart of an individual or in the hearts of a small group of people. He would call them to prayer. The brightness of the glory of God would begin to dispel the darkness in the days that followed. Mighty preachers would be raised out of nowhere. The Word of God would thunder forth in mighty power. Souls would be set aflame for the glory of God. Prayer initiated revival, and revival initiated prayer.

An apparent correlation exists between a movement of prayer and spiritual awakening. In some instances it is difficult to tell which came first. That is because spiritual awakening and prayer have the same focus: God. Revival is simply the manifest presence of God among His people. It is a special visitation of the Holy Spirit to His church.

True prayer is the method by which the Christian comes before the presence of God. Consequently, a praying

Christian will be a revived Christian, and a church that seeks the face of God will be one that knows the glory of God. Martyn Lloyd-Jones witnessed God's presence in his congregation in South Wales. He was a student of the great awakenings and revivalists of past days. He stated that the great need of the church is that of a knowledge of the glory of God. He said, "There is no doubt but that 99.9 percent of our troubles as Christians is that we are ignorant of God. We spend so much time in feeling our own pulse, taking our own spiritual temperature, considering our moods, and states and fears. Oh, if we but had some conception of Him, the inconceivable glory of God."[1]

The great need of the church in this generation is the manifest glory of God. We need men and women with the mark of God's glory upon their lives. Our pulpits need to be set aflame by men who have seen the King of glory in their secret chambers of prayer. Our pews need people to fill them whose hearts long for God's manifest presence in their lives. The need exists for men and women who are like Jesus because they have been with Jesus. Revival is when God is known as God of our lives, homes, churches, and communities.

Five major traits characterize the great historical awakenings. First, the awakenings were preceded by gross moral and spiritual declension in the church. The church ceased to be a great lighthouse for a world in a stormy sea and was drowning in the waves of immorality and impurity. Because her eyes were filled with impurities, she could not see God in His splendor and majesty.

Second, God would, at the darkest moment, breathe on the hearts of a few individuals. They would begin to seek His face, and a revival of prayer would result. The Holy Spirit would show men and women the utter necessity of absolute dependence upon God.

1. Martyn Lloyd-Jones, *Revival* (Westchester, Ill.: Crossway, 1987), p. 217.

Third, a visitation of God's presence would come among God's people. A fresh breath of life blew into the churches —the life of God in the hearts of His people. A new sense of purity of character grew among God's people. The church experienced the holiness of God, and Christians were conformed into the image of Christ.

Fourth, a reaping of a great evangelistic harvest occurred—a renewal of the preaching of the old truths of the Bible. Pastors and evangelists preached the holiness of God, the corrupted nature of man, and Christ as God's only provision for man's sin. They preached that Christ must be received by faith and that man must be born again. They preached against sin and set forth the extraordinary love of God. And God gave the increase. The greatest times of evangelism took place during the great spiritual awakenings.

Finally, growth in the church resulted, and new movements and ministers were thrust into world evangelism. There were lasting results; the fruit remained. Although there would be some excesses in each movement, in general the church would make great strides in building the kingdom of God.

One aspect of historical spiritual awakenings needs further study by Christians. The Bible exhorts the believer to remember the things that God has done for His people in past times. We have much to learn from the history of God's dealings with His people. Prayer will always be found at the root of those dealings. As a result, it would benefit us to look at the importance of prayer in historical awakenings. Although this is not an exhaustive study of spiritual awakenings, it will serve to remind us that God has not changed. The God of Paul, Peter, Whitefield, Wesley, Finney, and Moody is the God of our generation. He is looking for men and women who will take hold of Him in prayer and not let go until His glory comes.

EARLY CHURCH

The priority of spiritual awakening was so important that the Holy Spirit breathed on Luke to record His dealings with the early church. That first church was initiated and sustained by a prayer movement. The glory of God covered that early church.

Jesus told the disciples to wait in Jerusalem for the promise of the Father. The first call upon the New Testament church was prayer. Intense praying resulted in the powerful proclamation of Christ. In Acts 1:14 the church is found seeking the face of God: "These all with one mind were continually devoting themselves to prayer." In Acts 2:4-41 the church is empowered to proclaim the resurrection of Christ. Three thousand people were converted in this mighty visitation of God.

This incited the church to move forward in prayer. Acts 2:42 says, "They were continually devoting themselves to the apostles' teaching and to fellowship, to the breaking of bread and to prayer." The results were phenomenal. People came to know Christ daily. Peter and John are on their way to a prayer meeting in Acts 3, and five thousand are converted before they even arrive. The church continues to pray in Acts 4, which results in an even more powerful proclamation of the gospel. In Acts 5:14 they stop counting those who are being saved, simply stating, "All the more believers in the Lord, multitudes of men and women, were constantly added to their number."

This should be ample evidence of the relationship between prayer and the phenomenal growth of the New Testament church. But we should also look at the apostle Paul. Paul's ministry grew out of a prayer meeting. All of Europe and North America should be grateful for five humble men of prayer. The history of both continents would never be the same because of that prayer meeting, where a ministry was born that would ultimately shape much of Western civilization. The early church's motto was "pray and proclaim."

It was said of them that they were "men who have upset the world" (Acts 17:6).

THE FIRST GREAT AWAKENING

Two Britons and two North Americans were used of God during the first Great Awakening. George Whitefield began preaching outside the four walls of the church in England to the multitudes. John Wesley later joined Whitefield in this unique method of ministry. Thus, they became known as Methodists. Wesley and Whitefield had a profound impact on Britain and America. Untold thousands were converted to Christ, and the social and moral climates of both countries were greatly affected.

John Wesley was converted after attempting to be a missionary in America. He wrote in his diary on Tuesday, January 24, 1738, "I went to America to convert the Indians; but oh! who shall convert me?"[2] The answer to his question was found in a praying group of Germans called Moravians.

The leader of the Moravians was Count Ludwig von Zinzendorf. He stated, "My joy until I die . . . [is] to win souls for the Lamb."[3] Zinzendorf established a community called Herrnhut ("The Lord's Watch"), located in eastern Germany. A prayer meeting began and had far-reaching effects. These Moravians sought the Lord and cried unto Him for His power and presence. That prayer meeting lasted one hundred years, and out of it grew a missionary movement. The hearts of the Moravians were touched by the heart of God, which resulted in them developing a heart for the world.

Wesley had a "divine appointment" with some of those Moravians on board a ship for America. A great storm over-

2. Percy Parker, ed., *The Journal of John Wesley* (Chicago: Moody, n.d.), p. 53.
3. Lewis Drummond, *The Awakening That Must Come* (Nashville: Broadman, 1978), p. 74.

took them while they were at sea. The water split the main-sail in pieces and covered the ship. The English began to scream for their lives. However, the Moravians quietly worshiped God in the face of death. Wesley asked one afterward, "Were you not afraid?" He simply responded, "I thank God, no."[4]

John Wesley saw God on the faces of those dear praying people, and he never forgot what he saw. When he returned to England he visited the Moravians and had discussions with some of them. He attended a prayer meeting that the Moravians held at Aldersgate Street in London. Martin Luther's preface to the epistle to the Romans was read during that prayer meeting. Wesley described what transpired. He wrote, "About a quarter before nine, while he was describing the change which God works in the heart through faith in Christ, I felt my heart strangely warmed. I felt I did trust in Christ, Christ alone for salvation; and an assurance was given me that He had taken away my sins, even mine, and saved me from the law of sin and death."[5] That group of praying Germans lit a fire in Wesley that spread throughout Britain and extends today around the world. The forerunners of the revival in the 1700s were a band of praying men and women in Germany. They waited for the Lord at Herrnhut, and He visited His people.

THE GREAT AWAKENING OF 1857

The Great Awakening of 1857 was so profoundly affected by prayer that it was known to many as the revival of the prayer meeting. During 1857 financial panic occurred in America. Spiritual and moral decline had been on the rise for approximately seventeen years. God had used Charles Finney in years previous to the decline; however, economic greed and speculation had grown since that time.

4. Parker, p. 36.
5. Ibid., p. 64.

Jeremiah Lamphier began a noonday prayer meeting for laymen in downtown New York City on September 23, 1857. He sat alone for the first twenty-five minutes, but by 12:30 there were six men present. The following week twenty men attended. Within six months, more than ten thousand businessmen were attending. The Holy Spirit began to call people to pray. Many people were converted in the prayer meetings, and others found victory in their walk with God. It has been estimated that in America, "In just two years, over a million converts were added to the churches of all denominations. Over a million converts were added to the churches of Great Britain."[6] God wanted to bless His church, and the wind of the Spirit blew across the hearts of the people of God, calling them to prayer. Out of the prayer meetings grew a great harvest, and following the harvest grew great ministries. God raised up a shoe salesman, D. L. Moody, who would become one of the great evangelists of the world. Hudson Taylor, who would lead a great missionary movement, was ultimately affected by the revival. Men sought the Lord, He set them aflame, and nations were affected by the flames of revival.

THE WELSH REVIVAL

A young man named Evan Roberts was used as a mighty weapon of God during the Welsh Revival. But the instruments had to be broken, melted, and molded in order to be used of God. Seth Joshua told twenty-six-year-old Roberts not to miss the prayer meeting. During the spring of 1904, Roberts was awakened by the Holy Spirit at 1:00 A.M., and he communed with God for four hours. This continued steadily for approximately three months. God was desiring to bless the tiny nation of Wales, and He sought for a man who would yield himself to Him.

Not long after young Roberts heard Seth Joshua pray in a meeting, "Bend us, Lord." He stated that as he left, "I

6. Winkey Pratney, *Revival* (Springdale, Pa.: Whitaker, 1984), p. 158.

went out and I prayed, 'Oh, Lord, bend me.' "" God broke Evan Roberts. And He gave him a vision and a broken heart for his nation. Roberts began to ask God for one hundred thousand souls.

The Spirit of God descended upon the coal-mining country of Wales. J. Edwin Orr wrote of the impact that was made on the nation. He wrote, "Stocks of Welsh and English Bibles were sold out. Prayer meetings were held in coal mines, in trains and trams and places of business. . . . The magistrates in several places were presented with white gloves, signifying that there were utterly no cases to try. . . . Cursing and profanity were so diminished that several slow-downs were reported in the coal mines, for so many men gave up usual foul language that the pit ponies dragging the coal trucks in the mine tunnels did not understand what was being said to them and stood still, confused."[8]

Not only did God answer Roberts's prayer for one hundred thousand souls, but He multiplied the influence of the revival around the world. Men such as G. Campbell Morgan, Gipsy Smith, and F. B. Meyer were influenced by the revival. R. A. Torrey wrote an encouraging letter to Roberts stating his joy from hearing the reports of the movement of God. Reports of the revival spread throughout Europe, India, Asia, Australia, Africa, and North America. Evangelical Christianity would enter the twentieth century with the fires of revival spreading from Wales around the world. God found a young man who refused to miss the prayer meeting and cried unto the Lord, "Bend me, O God!"

A FINAL NOTE

The many other awakenings in church history have a common thread that runs throughout. Praying men and women have been used by God to ignite the flames of reviv-

---

7. Eifion Evans, *The Welsh Revival of 1904* (Wales, Great Britain: Evangelical Press of Wales, 1987), p. 69.
8. J. Edwin Orr, *The Flaming Tongue* (Chicago: Moody, 1975), p. 19.

al. God visited the Hebrides Islands three decades ago, which resulted in a great harvest. It began with two separate groups that prayed. And the story continues. When God gets ready to move, He calls men and women to prayer. The wind of God moves across the pages of the history of the church through praying saints.

The unusual revival which came to Asbury College early in 1970 and spread to scores of campuses across America is evidence that God is still at work in His world. . . . Perhaps the eruptions of revival which swept through a segment of our college youth in the early months of 1970 are harbingers of what the Holy Spirit is ready, able and willing to do, throughout the world, if Christians will dare to pay the price.

(Billy Graham, quoted in Robert E. Coleman,
One Divine Moment [Revell, 1970])

For the eyes of the Lord move to and fro throughout the earth that He may strongly support those whose heart is completely His.

(2 Chronicles 16:9)

12

Contemporary Awakenings and Prayer

God is not only the God of yesterday, but He is also the God of today. He is willing to manifest Himself to this generation or any future generation that will seek Him. Reading about His great deeds of past years is thrilling, but we must not forget that history is being made today. There is no difference between Luther, Wesley, Whitefield, Moody, or you and me. We were all formed from dust, and we shall return to dust. It is the life of God within us that gives us hope. His life not only gives us hope personally but also gives us hope for today. Christ can make a difference in this generation.

A few factors, however, are unique to this generation. For instance, we have the looming threat of a nuclear holocaust. We have crossed the line of scientific knowledge in the militarization of the world. Even if we could rid the world of all nuclear arsenals, the practical knowledge of nuclear weapons still exists in the minds of a multitude of scientists. We will never again be able to escape the threat of nuclear war.

We also face the potential of one of the greatest plagues known to mankind, acquired immunodeficiency syndrome (AIDS). The sexual revolution of the fifties and sixties has become the great tragedy of the eighties. Scientists frantically look for a medical solution to a moral and spiritual problem.

Economic and environmental problems are mounting around the world. Entire nations are gambling with their future by accumulating huge indebtedness. The ozone layer grows thinner. Famine threatens parts of the world.

Yet the church seems to be asleep. A hopeless world cries for some sign of light in the midst of darkness and desperation. This should be a time when the church is shining her brightest. The world needs to see the glory of God in the hearts of the people of God.

A few signs of hope exist in this generation. The Christian church is having phenomenal growth in certain areas of the world. Revival of historic proportion exists among certain groups of people today. These great movements of the Holy Spirit stand as a witness that God has not forgotten us. He is still on His throne and ready to manifest His glory upon those who will seek Him.

The great advances in the kingdom of God today are taking place in poorer nations of the world or in countries where Christians are persecuted. Many reasons contribute to this phenomenon; however, one factor cannot escape our attention. Where there is revival, a deep sense of need has preceded it. Need always drives people to prayer. Jesus came to the needy, hurting, and suffering segment of humanity. And so it is today.

Many Western evangelical Christians have refused to acknowledge their need. We have great programs to win the world but little power. We have beautiful buildings but empty pews. We have gained political clout but have lost our spiritual passion. The church in the West would do well to heed the message of the churches where revival exists. It is not enough to have information about revival; we must hunger and thirst for it. There must be an extraordinary prayer movement if we are to see the glory of God. It can no longer be business as usual. We must awaken from our slumber and seek the Lord.

Following are a few examples of the great things God is doing in this generation. They are not intended to be exhaustive, but they are a few places where God has allowed me to have contact. I have found the same thread woven into these contemporary revivals that existed in historical awakenings. That thread is the prayer factor. It is the missing factor from much of contemporary evangelical Christianity.

REVIVAL IN NAGALAND

Nagaland is located in the extreme eastern part of India, which borders Burma. The people come from Mongolian stock and have a historical background of animism and head-hunting. They are an agrarian people, and it is estimated that 60 percent of the population is illiterate. There are 1,200,000 Nagaland people, but only 800,000 live in the state of Nagaland.

Two spiritual awakenings have occurred among the Nagaland people in recent years. The first occurred in the early 1950s, and the second occurred from 1976 to 1979. In the early 1950s, there was a conflict between the Indian government and the people of Nagaland. The Indian government sent troops into Nagaland, because the natives were fighting for national independence. In 1953 missionaries were expelled.

When the unrest came to Nagaland in 1953, many people fled to the forests in fear for their lives. In their moment of desperation they cried to the Lord. The revival began with the Christians seeking the face of God with confession of sin and repentance. The revival fires became flames of evangelism, and many people were converted to Christ. The spirit of revival lasted until the late 1950s, then came an ebb in the flow of revival.

In 1976 the flames of awakening again began to burn brightly. A continuous spirit of revival existed through 1979. The Baptists had less than 100,000 adult members prior to the expulsion of the missionaries in 1953. It has been estimated that by 1980 there were 250,000 adult members of the Baptist churches and that 80 percent of the population had been converted to Christ.

One young leader from Nagaland told me how the revival had affected his life. On May 8, 1976, the fires of revival engulfed this young man's heart. One evening he went to meet some of his friends to go to a party. He was expecting them to come with wine; however, they came with new hearts filled with love for the Savior. His young friends asked him, "If you were to die tonight, do you know where you would spend eternity?" He struggled with the question. Later that night he received Christ. His heart was flooded with peace.

The next day at school two other young people came to know Jesus Christ. The Baptist school that he attended caught the fire of revival. Those young people began to talk about Christ during the break each day. More than three hundred students out of the one thousand enrolled in the school were converted to Christ at the break. As the revival spread, classes had to be canceled because of the outpouring of God's Spirit. Chapel services, which normally lasted forty-five minutes, were extended to two hours.

School normally ended at 2:00 P.M. When the revival came, however, students remained until 7:00 P.M. They held prayer meetings that lasted for several hours. They wept for souls. The revival then began to spread to the non-Christian schools. The students began to hold prayer meetings in the homes, which lasted until 1:00 A.M. Seven or eight non-Christians were converted nightly at these prayer meetings. Sometimes they would leave the prayer meetings and walk through the streets and neighborhoods proclaiming the gospel.

Even though there were no leaders, God moved among the students. The hardest sinners were converted to Christ.

The wine shops began to close because the young people no longer wanted to drink alcohol. Rock groups with names such as "Blood and Thunder," "Blood Suckers," and "The Rivals" were converted to Christ, and they became gospel-singing groups with names such as "The Living Gospel" and "Jesus Christ Revolution." The revival spread throughout the nation to other high schools and colleges.

Prayer was such a vital part of the revival movement that small buildings were erected next to many churches for houses of prayer. People came to these places to spend extended days in prayer and fasting.

The revival affected Nagaland in numerous ways. The characteristics of the revivals have been joyful praise, extraordinary prayer, deep repentance, and overflowing grace. Warring tribal groups made peace with one another and held joint worship services of reconciliation.

I asked one of the young Baptist leaders from Nagaland what he believed was the great need among Christians today. He responded, "We need to depend more upon God. He must be our starting point for everything. We must allow Him to set the agenda. Prayer is not when we bring our agendas to God. Prayer is coming before God and allowing Him to establish the agenda for our lives and ministries. Prayer begins with God and His will."

REVIVAL IN NORTHWEST ROMANIA

Several years ago I preached at a crusade in the Second Baptist Church of Oradea in Romania. During that crusade many came to know Jesus Christ as Lord and Savior. Many of the back pews were removed for the Sunday evening services because more people could be squeezed into the building if they stood during the services. More than three thousand people gathered to hear the message of Christ that evening, which was remarkable because that church did not even have Sunday evening services before the fires of revival came to that part of Romania.

Not only was the church filled with both Christians and non-Christians that Sunday evening, but the outside was completely surrounded by hungry listeners. People stood in the streets in subfreezing temperatures to hear the message of Christ. Every adjacent room was crowded.

A man came to me at the close of the service and asked what I thought about all that had transpired that evening. I was surprised that he did not know what God had done, but later I discovered that he had not been in the auditorium that evening. He had gathered with one hundred other men to pray for me while I preached. Another room was filled with one hundred women who were praying also. The glory of God was evident because the believers sought God.

Several years earlier it would have been difficult to imagine such a scene in that church. That church was like a sleeping giant. Then the church called Olah Liviu, a man of prayer, as their pastor.

One of the young professionals in the church told me about the early beginnings of the revival. When he was a child, Pastor Liviu would come to his home in the evening. Pastor Liviu and his father would pray late into the night. He said, "I remember lying in bed, and I could hear the pastor and my dad praying. They wept for souls. They continually asked God to send a mighty revival." God answered their prayers.

The pastor preached and taught the people to pray. Prayer and repentance were the themes that gripped the hearts of the people. The church entered into a covenant of repentance. There were more than two hundred conversions and public baptisms within the following six months. The revival fires were lit by two men who prayed.

Pastor Liviu eventually had to leave, and he emigrated to America. But the revival was not rooted in human personality. It began by people looking to God and would continue in the same manner. The church called Josif Ton as their pastor. Josif's ministry extended the revival to the intellectual community. Josif taught the Word of God to more than one thousand university students weekly. Josif was later exiled.

The leaders of the revival could be kept outside the borders of Romania, but the Originator of the revival could not be hindered. A spirit of prayer continues to prevail in the churches in the northwestern part of the nation. Although there are great difficulties and pressures from the government, the churches continue to experience phenomenal growth.

Revival at Asbury College

A pastor once told me that Korea is experiencing revival because its culture is conducive to spiritual awakening. He concluded that we do not have revival in North America and Western Europe because our societies operate on principles contrary to spiritual awakening. We live at too fast a pace. Others have questioned whether it is possible to experience revival in the Western world without some major catastrophe.

The revival at Asbury College in 1970, however, stands as one of the greatest signs of hope for spiritual awakening among evangelical Christians living in the West. Asbury College and Seminary are located in the small town of Wilmore, Kentucky, a few miles outside Lexington. No one would have expected that Wilmore would be the center of a minor awakening that would spread throughout college campuses in the United States and Canada.

Several months prior to the revival, different groups of students met together to pray for spiritual awakening. As time passed, a spirit of faith and expectancy grew among the students. No one anticipated, however, what would take place in the 10:00 A.M. chapel service on Tuesday, February 3, 1970. The dean of the college felt impressed by the Holy Spirit not to speak at chapel as originally planned. Instead, he opened the service for testimonies from the one thousand students gathered for the service. Something amazing happened in that service. God visited the students in mighty power. The chapel service that normally lasted for one hour was invaded by the presence of the Holy Spirit and lasted for 185 hours without interruption! At any time of the day or night, people could be found at the altar in prayer.

There was much confession of sin and much prayer. People began to hear about this phenomenal moving of the Holy Spirit at Asbury. They drove or flew to Lexington from throughout the United States. Many lives were transformed, and the revival began to spread to other campuses in the United States and Canada.

My own life was touched by the move of God at Asbury. I had the opportunity to speak there several weeks after the visitation of the Lord, and my heart was deeply touched by the lingering presence of the Holy Spirit on the campus. A friend of mine was a student at Southwestern Baptist Theological Seminary at that time. A team from Asbury was sent to Southwestern to give a report about the revival. My friend heard the students, and God gripped his heart. The experience resulted in heartfelt repentance and a new freshness in his walk with God.

Wherever the students from Asbury traveled, the same results accompanied them. Again, there was no leader. But God was with those students. Revival broke out at the Church of God College in Anderson, Indiana. I met a singing group from that college while I was preaching in a suburb of Washington, D.C. that summer. They had been set aflame by the revival at Asbury. A former drug addict who had been converted through the revival was with them. He brought many other drug addicts to the services, and they found the Savior also.

Because I saw the effects of the revival at Asbury, I am convinced that God is desiring to send a great spiritual awakening to the Western world. It is not our culture that prohibits revival in this generation. It is the prayerlessness of God's people. We must repent. Prayer is the forgotten factor in the life of the church in this generation.

A Final Word

Historical and contemporary awakenings serve as witnesses to the necessity of prayer. It is not the intent of this book, however, to merely give the reader more information about prayer. The church does not need to ask God, "Teach us *how to pray.*" We need to ask God, "Teach us *to pray.*"

Christians must set aside time, find a place, and quietly meet with God. The great need of this generation is for men and women who have met with God in the secret chamber of prayer.

I offer this simple work to those who would take up the challenge of spiritual awakening. There is a factor that can revolutionize our societies. It can turn sleepy, dead orthodoxy into living, dynamic, biblical Christianity. It can turn the heart of a nation to God Himself. It is a factor with which we must reckon our lives and our church communities. It is the prayer factor!